THE ONLY
GRAMMAR
BOOK
YOU'LL EVER NEED

A ONE-STOP SOURCE
FOR EVERY
WRITING ASSIGNMENT

SUSAN THURMAN

Edited by Larry Shea

⬛ ADAMS MEDIA
Avon, Massachusetts

Published by
Adams Media, a division of F+W Media, Inc.
57 Littlefield Street, Avon, MA 02322 U.S.A.
www.adamsmedia.com

ISBN 10: 1-58062-855-9
ISBN 13: 978-1-58062-855-6
Printed in the United States of America.

30 29 28 27 26

Library of Congress Cataloging-in-Publication Data
Thurman, Susan (Susan Sommers)
The only grammar book you'll ever need / Susan Thurman.
         p.   cm.
ISBN 1-58062-855-9
1. English language--Grammar--Handbooks, manuals, etc. I. Title.

PE1112 .T495 2003
428.2--dc21
                    2002153891

This publication is designed to provide accurate and authoritative information with regard to the subject matter covered. It is sold with the understanding that the publisher is not engaged in rendering legal, accounting, or other professional advice. If legal advice or other expert assistance is required, the services of a competent professional person should be sought.

—From a *Declaration of Principles* jointly adopted by a Committee of the American Bar Association and a Committee of Publishers and Associations

Many of the designations used by manufacturers and sellers to distinguish their products are claimed as trademarks. Where those designations appear in this book and Adams Media was aware of a trademark claim, the designations have been printed with initial capital letters.

This book is available at quantity discounts for bulk purchases.
For information, call 1-800-289-0963.

Contents

Introduction

"The Only Grammar Book You'll Ever Need."
Wow.

This book must be really good, mustn't it?

But before we tell you why this modestly titled volume really is the only grammar book you'll ever need, let's think about why you need a grammar book at all.

Maybe all that talk in English class about parts of speech and dangling participles never truly sunk in, even after your teacher covered the blackboard with those helpful sentence diagrams. (If English is not your first language, you might not even have had the benefit of such instruction.) Maybe you did know this material *once,* but many of the fine points of English grammar now give you trouble. Now you have to write something—a paper, a letter, a memo—for school, work, or your personal life. You might not be sure how to begin it, and you're definitely not confident about completing it correctly.

The Only Grammar Book You'll Ever Need explains the necessary terms for understanding and discussing grammar, the important rules and their exceptions, and all the most common writing errors—including how to avoid them.

This book can help you out in all types of writing situations, not just in formal assignments. Let's say you're rereading an e-mail you've composed (as you always do just before clicking "Send," right?). After reading this book, you'll find it much easier to notice and correct missing words, inappropriate language, unclear references, common misspellings, and more.

This may be the only grammar book you'll ever need, but it's not the only *book* you'll ever need for writing. A good dictionary (such as a hardcover college edition) is an essential desktop accessory, and a thesaurus can save you time when you're stumped looking for the right word. For certain types of work (especially academic writing), you may need one of the style guides listed in Chapter 10. But for solving tricky grammar questions, avoiding embarrassing errors, and getting your thoughts organized enough to put pen to paper, this compact work will provide you with all the tools you'll ever need.

Chapter 1

Finding the Right Words

The most damaging mistakes a writer can make are probably misspelling or misusing words. Just a few of these errors will make a reader lose confidence in what you're trying to say.

Here are the basic rules of English spelling and the most commonly misused words. For further help, Appendix A gives the correct spelling of hundreds of words that often confuse even the best spellers.

Spelling It Out

You probably remember this spelling rule from your elementary school:

> I before e,
> Except after c,
> Or when sounded as a,
> As in neighbor or weigh.

That's certainly a helpful rule—most of the time. It works for words such as *beige, ceiling, conceive, feign, field, inveigh, obeisance, priest, receive, shield, sleigh,* and *weight.*

But take a look at all these words: *ancient, being, caffeine, either, feisty, foreign, height, leisure, protein, reimburse, science, seize, society, sovereign, species, sufficient,* and *weird.*

There are an awful lot of exceptions, aren't there?

Here are some rules that generally apply to English nouns. Every rule will have an exception (and probably more than one), but these rules will provide you with some useful guidelines.

Forming Plurals of Nouns

1. To form the plural of most English words that don't end in *–s, –z, –x, –sh, –ch,* or *–ss,* add *–s* at the end:

▶ desk = desks, book = books, cup = cups

2. To form the plural of most English words that end in *–s, –z, –x, –sh, –ch,* and *–ss,* add *–es* at the end:

▶ bus = buses, buzz = buzzes, box = boxes, dish = dishes, church = churches, kiss = kisses

There are some exceptions to this rule that include *quizzes, frizzes,* and *whizzes.* (Note that the *–z* is doubled.)

3. To form the plural of some English words that end in *–o,* add *–es* at the end (this might now be known as the Quayle Rule):

▶ potato = potatoes, echo = echoes, hero = heroes, veto = vetoes

To make things interesting, for some other words that end in *–o,* add only *–s* at the end:

▶ auto = autos, alto = altos, two = twos, zoo = zoos, piano = pianos, solo = solos

And—just to keep you on your toes—some words ending in –*o* can form the plural in either way:

▶ buffalo = buffaloes/buffalos, cargo = cargoes/cargos, ghetto = ghettos/ghettoes

4. To form the plural of most English words that end in a consonant plus –*y*, change the *y* to *i* and add –*es:*

▶ lady = ladies, candy = candies, penny = pennies

5. To form the plural of most English words that end in a vowel plus –*y*, add –*s:*

▶ joy = joys, Monday = Mondays, key = keys, buy = buys

6. To form the plural of most English words that end in –*f* or –*fe*, change the *f* to *v* and add –*es:*

▶ knife = knives, leaf = leaves, wife = wives, wolf = wolves

Exceptions to this rule include *oaf, chef, cliff, belief, tariff, plaintiff, roof,* and *chief.* All simply add –*s* to form their plural.

7. Some words form their plurals in ways that defy categories:

▶ child = children, mouse = mice, foot = feet, person = people, tooth = teeth, ox = oxen

8. Foreign words, such as those of Greek or Latin origin, often have an irregular plural. In some cases, both the regular and irregular plural forms are acceptable.

▶ alumnus   alumni
▶ analysis   analyses
▶ focus   focuses or foci
▶ index   indexes or indices

9. Some words are the same in both singular and plural:
  ▶ deer, offspring, crossroads, headquarters, cod, series

Adding Prefixes and Suffixes

1. Words that end in –x don't change when a suffix is added to them:
  ▶ fax = faxing, hoax = hoaxed, mix = mixer

2. Words that end in –c don't change when a suffix is added to them if
the letter before the c is a, o, u, or a consonant:
  ▶ talc = talcum, maniac = maniacal

3. Words that end in –c usually add k when a suffix is added to them if
the letter before the c is e or i and the pronunciation of the c is hard:
  ▶ picnic = picnickers, colic = colicky, frolic = frolicking

4. Words that end in –c usually don't change when a suffix is added to
them if the letter before the c is e or i and the pronunciation of the c is
soft:
  ▶ critic = criticism, clinic = clinician, lyric = lyricist

5. Words that end in a single consonant that is immediately preceded
by one or more unstressed vowels usually remain unchanged before
any suffix:
  ▶ debit = debited, credit = creditor, travel = traveled

  Of course, there are exceptions, such as these:
  ▶ program = programmed, format = formatting, crystal = crystallize

6. When a prefix is added to form a new word, the root word usually
remains unchanged:
  ▶ spell = misspell, cast = recast, approve = disapprove

In some cases, however, the new word is hyphenated. These exceptions include when the last letter of the prefix and the first letter of the word it is joining are the same vowel; when the prefix is being added to a proper noun; and when the new word formed by the prefix and the root must be distinguished from another word spelled in the same way but with a different meaning:

▶ anti-institutional, mid-March, re-creation (versus recreation)

7. When adding a suffix to a word ending in *–y*, change the *y* to *i* when the *y* is preceded by a consonant:

▶ carry = carrier, irony = ironic, empty = emptied

Note that this rule doesn't apply to words with an *–ing* ending:

▶ carry = carrying, empty = emptying

This rule also doesn't apply to words in which the *–y* is preceded by a vowel:

▶ delay = delayed, enjoy = enjoyable

8. Two or more words that join to form a compound word usually keep the original spelling of each word:

▶ cufflink, billfold, bookcase, football, payday

9. If a word ends in *–ie*, change the *–ie* to *–y* before adding *–ing*:

▶ die = dying, lie = lying, tie = tying

10. When adding *–full* to the end of a word, change the ending to *–ful*:

▶ armful, grateful, careful, useful, colorful

The English Way

You probably know that the meanings of some words are different in Britain than in the United States, such as the British usage of *chips* for what Americans call *French fries,* and *lorry* for what Americans call a *truck.* But are you aware that there are many variations in spelling as well? Here are a few of the variations between American English and British English:

American	British	American	British
airplane	aeroplane	jail	gaol
center	centre	labor	labour
color	colour	spelled	spelt
draft	draught	theater	theatre
gray	grey	tire	tyre

Commonly Confused Words

Need a little advice (or should that be *advise*?) about certain words? Are you feeling alright (or *all right*?) about your ability to choose between (or is that *among*?) *alumni*, *alumnae*, *alumnus*, and *alumna*?

Not to worry! Here is a list of words often confused or misused, with an explanation of when each should be used.

a, an: *A* is used before words that begin with a consonant sound (*a* pig; *a* computer); *an* is used before words that begin with a vowel sound (*an* earring, *an* integer). The sound is what makes the difference. Write *a habit* because *habit* starts with the *h* sound after the article, but write *an honor* because the *h* in *honor* isn't pronounced.

▶ What an honor it is to meet a history expert like you.

a lot, alot, allot: Okay, let's begin with the fact that there is no such word as *alot*. If you mean a great number of people, use *a lot*. Here's a mnemonic for this: "a whole lot" is two whole words. If you mean *to allocate*, use *allot*. A mnemonic for *allot* is *all*ocate = *all*ot.

▶ Tomorrow night, the mayor will allot a lot of money for various municipal projects.

accept, except: *Accept* has several meanings, including *believe, take on, endure,* and *consent*; *except* means *excluding.* If your sentence can keep its meaning if you substitute *excluding*, use *except.*

▶ Except for food for the volunteers, Doris would not accept any donations.

adapt, adopt: To ad*a*pt is to ch*a*nge; to ad*o*pt is to take and make your *o*wn.

▶ After the couple adopted the baby, they learned to adapt to having little sleep.

advice, advise: *Advise* is what you do when you give *advice.* Here's a mnemonic to help you remember: To adv*ise* you must be w*ise.* Good adv*ice* is to drive slowly on *ice.*

▶ Grandpa tried to advise me when I was a youngster, but I wouldn't listen to his advice.

affect, effect: *Affect* is usually a verb (something that shows action), usually means *change* or *shape,* and—as a verb—has its accent on the first syllable. *Effect* is almost always a noun meaning *result* or *outcome, appearance* or *impression. (Effect* has a rare use as a verb, when it means *to achieve* or *cause.)*

▶ The effect of the announcement of impending war will not affect Adam's decision to join the military.

aggravate, annoy: If you mean *pester* or *irritate,* you want *annoy. Aggravate* means *exaggerate* or *make worse.*

▶ Steven was annoyed when his boss aggravated the situation by talking to the press.

aid, aide: If you help, you *aid*; if you have a helper or supporter, you have an aid*e*.
   ▶ The aid from my aide is invaluable.

all ready, already: If you mean all is ready, use *all ready*; if you mean in the past, use *already.*
   ▶ I already told you we're all ready to go out to dinner!

all right, alright: Although you often see the incorrect spelling *alright*, *all right* is always two words. You wouldn't say something is *aleft* or *alwrong*, would you? (Please say you wouldn't!)
   ▶ Is it all right with you if we eat in tonight?

all together, altogether: *All together* means *simultaneously* or *all at once*; *altogether* means *entirely* or *wholly.* If you can substitute *entirely* or *wholly* in the sentence and the meaning doesn't change, you need the form of the word that is entirely, wholly one word.
   ▶ You're altogether wrong about the six friends going all together to the dance; each is going separately.

alumni, alumnae, alumnus, alumna: Here's the rundown. One male graduate is an *alumnus*; one female graduate is an *alumna*; several female graduates are *alumnae*; and several male graduates or several male and female graduates are *alumni*. The short, informal form *alum* (or *alums*) can be used for any of the above.
   ▶ Although Mary Jo and her sisters are alumnae from Wellesley, Mary Jo is the alumna who receives the most attention; her brothers Martin and Xavier are alumni of Harvard, but Martin is a more famous alumnus than Xavier.

allusion, illusion: An *allusion* is a reference; an *illusion* is a false impression.

▶ Kay told Jerry that she was under the illusion he would be her Prince Charming; Jerry didn't understand the allusion.

altar, alter: If you chang*e* something, you alt*er* it; you worship before an *altar.*

▶ We'll alter the position of the altar so the congregation can see the new carvings.

among, between: Think division. If only two people are dividing something, use *between*; if more than two people are involved, use *among.* Here's a mnemonic: be*tw*een for *tw*o and among for a group.

▶ The money was divided between Sarah and Bob; the land was divided among Billy, Henry, and Janice.

anybody, any body: *Anybody* means *any one person* (and is usually interchangeable with anyone). *Any body* refers (pardon the graphic reference) to one dead person.

▶ Anybody can help to search for any body that might not have been found in the wreckage.

bad, badly: When you're writing about how you feel, use *bad.* However, if you're writing about how you did something or performed or reacted to something, use *badly* (twisted your ankle *badly*; played *badly* in the game).

▶ Gregg felt bad he had scored so badly on the test.

bear, bare: A b*ear* can t*ear* off your *ear*; if you're bar*e*, you're nud*e*.

▶ The bare bathers were disturbed when the grizzly bear arrived.

besides, beside: If you want the one that means *in addition to,* you want the one that has an additional *s* (*besides*); *beside* means *by the side of.*

▶ Besides her groom, the bride wanted her dad beside her in the photo.

breath, breathe: You take a single *breath*; you inhal*e* and *e*xhal*e* when you breath*e*.

▶ In the cold of the winter, it was hard for me to breathe when taking a breath outside.

can, may: If you *can* do something, you're physically able to do it. If you *may* do it, you have permission to do it.

▶ You can use *ain't* in a sentence, but you may not.

cannot, am not, is not, are not, and all other "nots": For some strange reason, *cannot* is written as one word. All other words that have *not* with them are written as two words. Go figure.

capital, capitol: The *capitol* is the building in which the legislative body meets. If you mean the one in Washington, D.C., use a capital *C;* if you mean the one in your state, use a lowercase *c.* Remember that the building (the one spelled with an *o*) usually has a dome. Use *capital* with all other meanings.

▶ The capital spent by the legislators at the capitol is appalling.

carat, caret, carrot, karat: A *carat* is a weight for a stone (a diamond, for instance); *carat* is also an alternate spelling of *karat*, which is a measurement of how much gold is in an alloy (as in the abbreviation 18k; the *k* is for *karat).* A *caret* is this proofreading mark: ^ (meaning that you should insert something at that point). Finally, a *carrot* is the orange vegetable your mother told you to eat.

▶ Set in an eighteen-karat gold band, the five-carat diamond was shaped like a carrot.

cite, sight, site: Your *sight* is your vision or a view (you use your *sight* to look at a beautiful *sight*); to *c*ite is to make referen*c*e to a spe-*c*ific sour*c*e; a *site* is a location, such as on the Internet.

▶ The colors on the Web site you cited in your paper were a sight to behold.

coarse, course: If something is *coarse*, it's rough; *oars* are c*oars*e. A c*ou*rse is a r*ou*te, a class, or part of the idiomatic phrase "of course."

▶ The racecourse led the runners over coarse terrain.

complement, compliment: If something completes another thing, it *complements* it (*comple*te = *comple*ment). If you receive praise, you've gotten a *compliment* (*I* like to receive a compl*i*ment).

▶ The jewelry will complement the outfit the star will wear, and she will surely receive many compliments on her attire.

council, counsel: A *council* is an official group, a committee; to *counsel* is to give advice (the stockbroker coun*sel*ed me to *sel*l).

▶ The town council decided to counsel the youth group on the proper way to ask for funds.

desert, dessert: A *desert* is a dry, arid place or (usually used in the plural form) deserved reward or punishment (just *deserts*). The verb that means *to leave* is also *desert*. The food that is *s*o *s*weet is a de*ss*ert.

▶ While lost in the desert, Rex craved a dessert of apple pie à la mode.

discreet, discrete: *Discreet* means *cautious*, *careful*, or *guarded in conduct*. (Be discre*et* about whom you m*eet*.) *Discrete* means *separate* or *disconnected*.

▶ The dancer's discreet movements were discrete from those performed by the rest of the chorus.

dual, duel: The first means *two* (*dual* purposes); the second is a fight or contest (the lover's jealousy was f*uel* for the d*uel*).

▶ There were dual reasons for the duel: revenge and money.

emigrate, immigrate: To *e*migrate is to *e*xit a country; to *i*mmigrate is to come *i*nto a country.

▶ Ten people were trying to emigrate from the tyranny of their country and immigrate to the United States.

ensure, insure: To *ensure* is to *make certain of something*; *insure* is used only for business purposes (to *insure* a car).

▶ To ensure that we continue to insure your house and car, send payment immediately.

envelop, envelope: If you wra*p* something, you envelo*p* it; the paper container that you use for your letter is an *envelope*.

▶ The hidden purpose of the envelope was to envelop the two sticks of candy that were mailed to me.

everyday, every day: *Everyday* means *routine* or *daily* (*everyday* low cost); *every day* means *every single day* (low prices *every day*). Use *single* words if you mean every *single* day.

▶ The everyday inexpensive prices of the store meant that more shoppers came every day.

faze, phase: To *faze* is to *intimidate* or *disturb*. As a noun, a *phase* is *a period of time*; as a verb, it means *to establish gradually*.

▶ I wasn't fazed by his wish to phase out our relationship.

fewer, less: Use *fewer* to describe plural words; use le*ss* to describe *s*ingular words.

▶ The new product has fewer calories, but less fat.

forego, forgo: If you mean something that has gone be*fore*, use *fore*go (a *foregone* conclusion); if you want the word that means *to do without something*, use *forgo* (the one that is without the *e*).

▶ It's a foregone conclusion that Meg and Marion will forgo sweets when they're dieting.

foreword, forward: The word that means *the opening information in a book* is *foreword* (it comes be*fore* the first important *word* of the book); for any other meaning, use *forward*.

▶ To gain insight into the author's intent, you should read the foreword before you proceed forward in the book.

good, well: *Good* is an adjective; it does not mean in *a high-quality manner*, or *correctly*. If you want either of those meanings you need an adverb, so you want *well*.

▶ You did well on the test; your grade should be good.

hear, here: You h*ear* with your *ear*. *Here* is the opposite of *t*here.

▶ Did you hear that Aunt Lucy is here?

hopefully: If you mean *I hope*, or *it is hoped*; then that's what you should write. *Hopefully* means *confidently* or *with anticipation*.

▶ The director waited hopefully for the Oscar nominations to be announced.

imply, infer: Both of these have to do with words not said aloud. A *s*peaker im*p*lies something; a liste*n*er i*n*fers something.

▶ Rufus thought the boss had implied that she would be back for an inspection next week, but Ruth did not infer that.

in, into: *In* means with*in*; *into* means from the outside *to* the *in*side.
> ▶ Go into the house, go in my purse, and bring me money.

its, it's: *It's* means only *it is* (before *it's* too late); *its* means *belonging to it* (I gave the dog *its* food and water).
> ▶ It's a shame that the dog lost its bone.

lay, lie: Now I *lay* my head on the pillow; last night I *laid* my head on the pillow; in the past I have *laid* my head on the pillow. If it helps to remember the difference, the forms of *lay* (meaning *to put or place*) are transitive (they take an object). Today I *lie* in the sun; yesterday I *lay* in the sun; in the past I have *lain* in the sun. The forms of *lie* (meaning *to rest or recline*) are intransitive (they take no object).
> ▶ As I lay in bed, I wondered where I had laid my watch.

loose, lose: *Loose* (which rhymes with *noose*) means *not tight*. *Lose* is the opposite of *find*.
> ▶ Will I lose my belt if it's too loose?

may of, might of, must of, should of, would of, could of: When we speak, we slur these phrases so that they all sound as if they end in *of*, but in fact all of them end in *have*. Their correct forms are *may have*, *might have*, *must have*, *should have*, *would have*, and *could have*.
> ▶ I must have thought you would have been able to find the room without any directions.

pair, pear: The first has to do with two (*pair* of pandas; to *pair* up for the dance); the second is a fruit (you *eat* a p*ear*).
> ▶ The romantic pair bought a pear to share on the picnic.

passed, past: *Passed* is a verb; *past* is an adjective (p*ast* often means l*ast*) or noun meaning *the preceding time.*

▶ In the past, twenty Easter parades have passed down this street.

peak, peek, pique: A *peak* is a *high point*, like a mountain peak (think of the shape of the *A* in PE*A*K); to p*ee*k at something is to try to s*ee* it; to *pique* is to *intrigue* or *stimulate.*

▶ Dan tried to pique Lora's interest in climbing by telling her that she could peek through the telescope when they reached the mountain's peak.

pore, pour: If you *read something carefully*, you *pore* over it. If you make a liquid go *ou*t of a container, you p*ou*r it.

▶ After Harry accidentally poured ink on the new floor, he pored over several books to find out how to clean the stain.

principle, principal: *Principle* means *law* or *belief. Principal* means *major* or *head*; it also means *money that earns interest in a bank.* The princi*pal* is the head person in a school; he or she is your *pal* and makes princi*pal* decisions.

▶ That is the most important principle our principal believes.

quiet, quite: *Quiet* is *calm* or *silence*; *quite* means *to a certain extent.* Be sure to check the ending of the word you use; that's where mistakes are made. You can think of being as qui*et* as *E.T.* visiting Earth.

▶ Are you quite sure that you were quiet in the library?

real, really: *Real* means *actual* or *true*; *really* means *in truth* or *in reality.* Except in the most casual tone in writing, neither *real* nor *really* should be used in the sense of *very* (that's a *real* good song on the radio; I'm *really* glad that you tuned to that station).

▶ When I realized I was really lost, the real importance of carrying a compass hit me.

set, sit: If you pla*c*e something, you s*e*t it. If you're in an upr*i*ght position (like in a chair), you s*i*t. In addition, *set* is a transitive verb (it must have an object); *sit* is an intransitive verb (it doesn't have an object).

▶ Please set the table before you sit down.

stationery, stationary: If you mean something that lacks motion, use *stationary*; if you mean something to write a lett*e*r on, use *stationery*.

▶ The stationery store had a picture of people riding stationary bicycles.

supposed (to): Often the –*d* is incorrectly omitted from *supposed to* (meaning *expected to* or *designed to*).

▶ In this job, you are supposed to be able to write clear and effective memos.

than, then: If you mean *next* or *therefore* or *at that time*, you want *then*. If you want the word that shows a comp*a*rison, use th*a*n.

▶ For a while, Mary ran more quickly than I; then she dropped her pace.

that, which: For clauses that don't need commas (restrictive clauses), use *that*. For nonrestrictive clauses, which need commas, use *which*.

▶ The local dog kennels, which are on my way to work, are the ones that have been featured in the news lately.

there, their, they're: If you want the opposite of *here*, use t*here*; if you mean they a*re*, you want they'*re*; if you mean belonging to *them*, use *their*.

▶ There are the employees who think they're going to get their ten percent raises tomorrow.

to, too, two: If you mean something *additional*, it's the one with the *additional o (too)*; *two* is the *number after one*; *to* means *in the direction of something.*

▶ Did our supervisor ask the two new employees to go to Detroit and Chicago, too?

troop, troupe: Both are groups of people, but *troupe* refers to actors only.

▶ The troupe of actors performed for the troop of Brownies.

try and, try to: Almost always the mistake comes in writing *try and* when you need to use *try to.*

▶ The lady said she would try to get the dress in my size; I hoped she would try and keep looking.

use to, used to: *Use to* means *employ for the purposes of*; *used to* (often misspelled without the *–d*) means *formerly* or *in the past.*

▶ I used to like to listen to the excuses people would use to leave work early.

who, which, that: Don't use *which* when you're writing about people.

▶ The federal inspector, who gives the orders that we all must obey, said that the environmental protection law, which had never been enforced, would result in higher costs.

whose, who's: *Whose* means *belonging to whom*; *who's* is short for *who is* (the apostrophe means the *i* has been omitted).

▶ After the sock hop, who's going to determine whose shoes these are?

your, you're: If you mean *belonging to you*, use *your* (this is *our* car; that is y*our* car); if you mean *you are*, use *you're* (remember that the apostrophe means the *a* has been omitted).

▶ If you're going to Florida, be sure to put some sunscreen on your face.

No Such Word

Some words and phrases don't make our list of commonly confused words because they aren't proper words at all. These are the nonstandard usages that you often won't find in the dictionary and that you shouldn't—ever—use in your own writing. Such words and phrases include *anyways, can't hardly, can't help but, can't scarcely, everywheres, hisself, irregardless, nowheres, off of, theirselves, theirself,* and—let's not forget—*ain't.*

Chapter 2

Parts of Speech

Why on earth would anyone other than an English teacher be interested in the parts of speech, you may be wondering.

The parts of speech provide the essential vocabulary for discussing grammar and good writing. Throughout this book—and in real life—you'll encounter choices concerning verb tenses (*was going* or *went*?), pronoun cases (*they* or *them*?), or capitalization of nouns (*senator* or *Senator*?). If you don't know what verbs, pronouns, and nouns even are, you won't get far in learning to pick the right word for each situation.

Nouns

A **noun** simply gives the name of a person *(Sammy, man)*, place *(Philadelphia, city)*, thing *(Toyota, car)*, or idea *(philosophy, warmth, love)*.

You'll notice that some of the nouns mentioned in the previous paragraph are capitalized and some are not. **Proper nouns** (particular persons, places, things, or ideas) are capitalized, whereas **common nouns** (everyday names of persons, places, things, or ideas) are not.

Proper Noun	Common Noun
February	month
Egypt	country
Mrs. Davis	teacher

Nouns are divided into several other categories. **Concrete nouns** name things that can be seen, felt, heard, touched, or smelled (*star, water, album, television, flower*). **Abstract nouns** name concepts, beliefs, or qualities (*freedom, capitalism, courage*). **Compound nouns** consist of more than one word, but count as only one noun (*Franklin County Community and Technical College*).

Count nouns are persons, places, or things that can be (surprise!) counted (three *cars*, seventy-six *trombones*); **noncount nouns** cannot be counted (*unease, happiness*) and are always singular.

Collective nouns are sometimes counted as one unit (that is, considered to be singular) and sometimes counted separately (that is, considered to be plural). *Army, herd, pack,* and *family* are all collective nouns.

In a sentence, a noun will act either as a subject or some type of complement (predicate nominative, direct or indirect object of a verb, or object of a preposition). Chapter 3, on basic sentence structure, defines those terms and gives examples for each.

Pronouns

The textbook definition of a **pronoun** is "a word that takes the place of a noun." Okay, just what does that mean? Read this paragraph.

▶ When Mrs. Anne Marie Schreiner came into the room, Mrs. Anne Marie Schreiner thought to Mrs. Anne Marie Schreiner's self, "Is the situation just Mrs. Anne Marie Schreiner, or is the temperature really hot in here?" Mrs. Anne Marie Schreiner went to the window and opened the lower part of the window, only to have a number of mosquitoes quickly fly right at Mrs. Anne Marie Schreiner. Mrs. Anne Marie Schreiner said a few choice words, and then Mrs. Anne Marie Schreiner began swatting the pesky mosquitoes, managing to hit a few of the mosquitoes when the mosquitoes came to rest on Mrs. Anne Marie Schreiner's arm.

Isn't that the most irritating paragraph you've ever read? Now read the same paragraph, but with pronouns inserted in the right places:

▶ When Mrs. Anne Marie Schreiner came into the room, she thought to herself, "Is it just me, or is it really hot in here?" She went to the window and opened the lower part of it, only to have a number of mosquitoes quickly fly right at her. She said a few choice words, and then she began swatting the pesky mosquitoes, managing to hit a few of them when they came to rest on her arm.

What a difference a few pronouns make!

Types of Pronouns

To figure out which type a pronoun is (some pronouns can be more than one), look at the way the word is used in the sentence.

1. **Personal pronouns** represent people or things: *I, me, you, he, him, she, her, it, we, us, they, them.*
   ▶ I came to see you and him today.

2. **Possessive pronouns** show ownership (possession): *mine, yours, hers, his, theirs, ours.*

▶ "These parking spaces are yours; ours are next to the door," the teachers explained to the students.

3. **Demonstrative pronouns** demonstrate or point out someone or something: *this, that, these, those.*
   ▶ This is his umbrella; that is your umbrella.

4. **Relative pronouns** relate one part of the sentence to another: *who, whom, which, that, whose.*
   ▶ The man whom I almost hit last night works in this shop. (*Whom* relates back to *man.*)

   ▶ One country that I'd like to visit someday is France. (*That* relates to *country.*)

5. **Reflexive pronouns** (sometimes called **intensive** pronouns) reflect back to someone or something else in the sentence: *myself, yourself, himself, herself, itself, ourselves, yourselves, themselves.*
   ▶ You must ask yourself what you would do in such a situation. (*Yourself* relates back to *you.*)

6. **Interrogative pronouns** interrogate (ask a question): *who, whom, which, whose, what.*
   ▶ What in the world was that politician talking about?

7. **Indefinite pronouns**, contrary to their label, sometimes refer to a definite (specific) person, place, or thing that has already been mentioned in the sentence. Indefinite pronouns include *all, another, any, anybody, anyone, anything, both, each, either, everybody, everyone, everything, few, many, most, much, neither, no one, nobody, none, nothing, one, other, others, several, some, somebody, someone,* and *something.*

Keep in mind that *all, any, more, most, none,* and *some* sometimes are singular and sometimes are plural.

To learn how to always choose correctly from this multitude of pronouns, see Chapter 5.

Adjectives

The textbook definition of an **adjective** is "a word that modifies a noun or pronoun."

▶ The framed picture came crashing off the wall during the recent earthquake.

Framed gives you information about *picture*, and *picture* is a thing (a noun), so *framed* must be an adjective.

Another method of checking for an adjective is to ask yourself if the word you wonder about answers one of these questions:

- Which one?
- What kind of?
- How many?

You can see that *framed* answers both *which one?* (which picture? the framed one) and *what kind?* (what kind of picture? the framed one), so it must be an adjective.

A special category of adjectives—**articles**—consists of just three words: *a, an,* and *the. A* and *an* are called indefinite articles because they do not indicate anyone or anything specific *(a house, an honor)*; *the* is called a definite article (actually, it's the only definite article) because it does name someone or something specific *(the owl, the transit system).*

Another subcategory of adjectives is called **determiners**. These are adjectives that make specific the sense of a noun; they help determine to which particular units the nouns are referring (e.g., *the country*, *those apples*, *seven pencils*).

When trying to figure out if a word is an adjective, look at the way the word is used in the sentence. Take a look at these sentences:

▶ The tense situation became much more relaxed when the little boy arrived.

▶ What is the tense of that verb?

In the first sentence, *tense* describes *situation* (a thing), so it's an adjective. In the second sentence, *tense* is a thing, so it's a noun.

Verbs

A **verb** is defined as "a word that expresses action or being." Verbs that express action are **action verbs**. Action verbs are the most common verbs, and they are easy to spot. For example:

▶ Marilyn jumped for joy when Frank called her.

(*Jumped* and *called* both show action.)

Action verbs can be divided into two categories: **transitive** and **intransitive**. The textbook definition of a transitive verb is "a verb that takes an object." What does that mean? If you can answer *whom?* or *what?* to the verb in a sentence, then the verb is transitive.

▶ I carried the injured boy to the waiting ambulance.

Carried whom or what? Since *boy* answers that question, the verb *carried* is transitive in that sentence.

▶ Exhausted after a hard day's work, I sank into the sofa with great delight.

Sank whom or what? Nothing in the sentence answers that, so the verb *sank* is intransitive in that sentence.

Knowing about transitive and intransitive verbs can help you with some easily confused verbs, such as *lie* and *lay*, and *sit* and *set*. You'll be able to see that *lie* is intransitive (I lie down), *lay* is transitive (I lay the book on the table), *sit* is intransitive (I'll sit here for a while), and *set* is transitive (Mary Beth set the vase on the dresser).

"Being" Verbs

Granted, the action verb is easy to spot. But what in the world is meant by the part of the definition that says a verb "expresses . . . being"? That usually means that the word is a form of the verb *be*.

Here are the forms of *be* (except for *been* and *being*, not one of them looks like *be*): *am*, *is*, *are*, *was*, *were*, *be*, *being*, *been*. These forms also include *has been*, *should have been*, *may be*, and *might be*.

▶ I am sitting on the dock of the bay.
(*am* is a present tense form of *be*)

▶ Yesterday she was sitting on the dock of the bay.
(*was* is a past tense form of *be*)

Linking Verbs

Just to complicate the situation, the words in the following list are sometimes action verbs and sometimes **linking verbs** (depending on when you went to school, you may know them as copulative verbs).

appear	feel	look	remain	smell	stay
become	grow	prove	seem	sound	taste

So when do these twelve verbs act as action verbs, and when are they linking verbs? Use this test: If you can substitute a form of *be* (*am*, *is*, *was*, and so on) and the sentence still makes sense, by golly, you've got yourself a linking verb. Look at these examples.

▶ The soup tasted too spicy for me.

Substitute *was* or *is* for *tasted* and you have this sentence:
▶ The soup was (is) too spicy for me.

It makes perfect sense. Now look at this one:
▶ I tasted the spicy soup.

Substitute *was* or *is* for *tasted* and you have this sentence:
▶ I was (is) the spicy soup.

It doesn't make much sense, so you don't have a linking verb.

Helping (Auxiliary) Verbs

Another type of verb that may occur in a sentence is a **helping** or **auxiliary verb.** It can join the main verb (becoming the helper of the main verb) to express the tense, mood, and voice of the verb. Common helping verbs are *be*, *do*, *have*, *can*, *may*, and so on. (The first two sentences of this paragraph have helping verbs: *may* and *can*.)

The Principal Parts of Verbs

The phrase "the principal parts of verbs" refers to basic forms that verbs can take. In English there are four principal parts: the present infinitive (which you see as the main entry in a dictionary), the past tense, the past participle, and the present participle. Take a look at the principal parts of these verbs:

You'll note that the first three examples all form their past and past participle by adding –*d* or –*ed* to the present infinitive. Most English verbs do this; they are called **regular verbs**. The last three examples, however, are not formed in the regular way; these are called (surprise!) **irregular verbs**. All verbs form the present participle by adding *–ing* to the present infinitive.

In Chapter 4, you'll learn more about how to properly use the many types of verbs.

Present Infinitive	Past Tense	Past Participle	Present Participle
turn	turned	turned	turning
scratch	scratched	scratched	scratching
hammer	hammered	hammered	hammering
bring	brought	brought	bringing
broadcast	broadcast	broadcast	broadcasting
rise	rose	risen	rising

Adverbs

An **adverb** is a word that modifies (describes, gives more information about) a verb, adjective, or other adverb.

▶ Yesterday the quite relieved soldier very quickly ran out of the woods when he saw his comrade frantically waving at him.

The adverbs in that sentence are *yesterday* (modifies the verb *ran*), *quite* (modifies the adjective *relieved*), *very* (modifies the adverb *quickly*), *quickly* (modifies the verb *ran*), and *frantically* (modifies the verb *waving*).

If you still need help finding adverbs, try this. Ask yourself if the word you're wondering about answers one of these questions:

- How?
- When?
- Where?
- Why?
- Under what circumstances?
- How much?
- How often?
- To what extent?

In the example above, *yesterday* answers the question *when?*; *quite* answers the question *to what extent?*; *very* answers the question *to what extent?* (or *how much?*); *quickly* answers the question *how?* (or *to what extent?*); and *frantically* answers the question *how?*

Conjunctive Adverbs

Conjunctive adverbs are in a category of their own. These words join independent clauses into one sentence. (You'll also see them in lists of transitional words and phrases.) Some examples:

accordingly	furthermore	instead	next
also	hence	likewise	otherwise
besides	however	meanwhile	still
consequently	incidentally	moreover	therefore
finally	indeed	nevertheless	thus

Use conjunctive adverbs to join short sentences into more complex thoughts; however (did you notice the conjunctive adverb there?), be sure that:

1. You have a complete thought on either side of the conjunctive adverb.
2. You put a semicolon before it and a comma after it.
3. You're joining two closely related thoughts.
4. You've used the right conjunctive adverb.

A small group of adverbs known as **intensifiers** or **qualifiers** (*very* is the most common intensifier) increase the intensity of the adjectives and other adverbs they modify. Other common intensifiers are *awfully, extremely, kind of, more, most, pretty* (as in *pretty happy*), *quite, rather, really* (as in *really sad*), *somewhat, sort of,* and *too.*

Comparisons with Adjectives and Adverbs

Sometimes you need to show how something compares with or measures up to something else. You may want to let your friends know if a new scary movie you've seen is *scarier* than another one you've all recently watched together or perhaps even the *scariest* movie you've ever seen.

In writing comparisons, you can use one of three different forms (called degrees) of adjectives and adverbs:

- The **positive degree** simply makes a statement about a person, place, or thing.
- The **comparative degree** compares two (but only two) people, places, or things.
- The **superlative degree** compares more than two people, places, or things.

Positive	Comparative	Superlative
blue	bluer	bluest
dirty	dirtier	dirtiest
happy	happier	happiest
tall	taller	tallest

Here are a couple of rules to help you in forming the comparative and superlative:

Rule #1. One-syllable adjectives and adverbs usually form their comparative form by adding *–er* and their superlative form by adding *–est*. (See the examples *tall* and *blue* in the table.)

Rule #2. Adjectives of more than two syllables and adverbs ending in *–ly* usually form comparative forms by using *more* (or *less*) and superlative forms by using *most* (or *least*).

Positive	Comparative	Superlative
awkwardly	more awkwardly	most awkwardly
comfortable	more comfortable	most comfortable
qualified	less qualified	least qualified

Rule #3. Confusion sometimes takes place in forming comparisons of words of two syllables only. Here's the rub: Sometimes two-syllable words use the *–er*, *est* forms, and sometimes they use the *more*, *most* (or *less*, *least*) forms.

Positive	Comparative	Superlative
sleepy	sleepier	sleepiest
tiring	more tiring	most tiring

So how do you know whether to use the *–er*, *est* form or the *more*, *most* form? You have to use a dictionary (a large dictionary, not a paperback one) if you're not sure. If there are no comparative or superlative forms listed in the dictionary, then use the *more*, *most* form.

There are a few exceptions to the above rules; these include:

Positive	Comparative	Superlative
bad	worse	worst
far	farther/further	farthest/furthest
good	better	best
well	better	best
ill	worse	worst
little	littler/less/lesser	littlest/least
many	more	most
much	more	most
old (persons)	elder	eldest
old (things)	older	oldest

One common mistake in both writing and speaking is to use the superlative form when the comparative should be used. Remember that if you're comparing two persons, places, or things, you use only the comparative form (not the superlative). Look at this sentence:

▶ Of my two dogs, the cocker spaniel is the friendliest.

The comparison is between only two *(two dogs)*, so the sentences should be written with the comparative form *(friendlier)* instead of the superlative.

Another frequent mistake in comparisons is to use both the *–er* and *more* or *–est* and *most* forms with the same noun, as in *the most tallest statue* or *a more happier child*. Remember that one form is the limit. In the examples, *most* and *more* need to be eliminated.

Because some comparisons can be interpreted more than one way, be sure that you include all the words necessary to give the meaning you intend. Read this sentence:

▶ In the long jump, Adele could beat her rival Fern more often than her teammate Sherry.

When the sentence is constructed that way, it isn't clear if the meaning is the following:

▶ In the long jump, Adele could beat her rival Fern more often than her teammate Sherry could.

or

▶ In the long jump, Adele could beat her rival Fern more often than she could beat her teammate Sherry.

Prepositions

A **preposition** is a word that links a noun or pronoun to some other word in a sentence. Take, for example, these short sentences:

▶ Jack and Jill went up the hill.

(*Up* is a preposition connecting *went* and *hill.*)

▶ Little Jack Horner sat in a corner.
(In is a preposition connecting sat and corner.)

Following are the most common prepositions.

about	behind	down	off	to
above	below	during	on	toward
across	beneath	except	onto	under
after	beside	for	out	underneath
against	between	from	outside	until
along	beyond	in	over	up
among	but	inside	past	upon
around	by	into	since	with
at	concerning	like	through	within
before	despite	of	throughout	without

Here's one way of remembering what a preposition is. Look at the last eight letters of the word *preposition*; they spell *position*. A preposition sometimes tells the position of something: *in, out, under, over, above,* and so forth.

You've heard the rule about never ending a sentence with a preposition, haven't you? Generally, your writing does sound better if you can structure a sentence so that you don't end with a preposition. However, sometimes you want a more colloquial or conversational tone, and—let's face it—in speaking, we often end sentences with prepositions. Would you be likely to say:

▶ With whom are you going to the party?
or
▶ Whom are you going to the party with?

The second way (with the preposition at the end) is almost always the way the sentence normally is said. (In fact, speakers usually use *who* instead of *whom* in a sentence like this, but you can read about that mistake in Chapter 5.)

Conjunctions

A **conjunction** joins words in a sentence; that is, it provides a junction between words. Conjunctions are divided into three categories:

1. Coordinating conjunctions include *but, or, yet, so, for, and*, and *nor*. You might want to remember them by using the mnemonic word *boysfan*.

2. Correlative conjunctions cannot stand alone; they must have a "relative" nearby, usually in the same sentence. The pairs include *both/and, either/or, neither/nor, not only/also,* and *not only/but also*.

3. Subordinating conjunctions are used in the beginning of dependent clauses (words that have a subject and verb but which cannot stand alone as sentences). You may remember that dependent clauses are sometimes called subordinate clauses. The most common ones are the following:

after	before	providing that	when
although	even though	since	whenever
as if	how	so long as	where
as in	if	so that	wherever
as long as	in order that	than	whether
as much as	in that	that	while
as soon as	inasmuch as	though	
assuming that	now that	unless	
because	once	until	

Interjections

Egad! You don't remember what an **interjection** is? It's a word that can either express surprise or some other kind of emotion, or it can be used as filler. Interjections often stand alone. If one is part of a sentence, it doesn't have a grammatical relation to the other words in the sentence; if it's taken out, the meaning of the sentence will be unchanged. Take a look at these sentences:

▶ Hey, what's going on?
▶ Well, I don't know what to say.
▶ Ouch! Did you step on my toe?

Hey, *well*, and *ouch* are interjections.

When you're expressing a strong emotion or surprise (as in *Stop!* or *Darn it all!*), use an exclamation point. If you're using milder emotion or merely using a filler (as in *like* or *well*), use a comma.

A note of caution about interjections: Use them in moderation, if at all. In dialogue, interjections are used far more often than in more formal writing (where they are hardly ever used).

Chapter 3

Basic Sentence Structure

By definition, every sentence must have the following: (1) a predicate (usually called a verb) and (2) the subject of that verb, and (3) the words must contain a complete thought.

In this chapter, we'll consider what makes a sentence complete and how to identify its elements: subjects, direct objects, prepositional phrases, subordinate clauses, and all the rest. After a look at different types and functions of sentences, we'll tackle the most troublesome aspect for many writers: getting the subject and verb to agree.

Subjects and Predicates

The **complete subject** is the person, place, or thing that the sentence is about, along with all the words that modify it (describe it or give more information about it). The **complete predicate** (verb) is what the person, place, or thing is doing, or what condition the person, place, or thing is in.

Complete Subject	Complete Predicate (Verb)
The aged, white-haired gentleman	walked slowly down the hall.

The **simple subject** of a sentence is the fundamental part of the complete subject—the main noun(s) and pronoun(s) in the complete subject. In this example, the simple subject is *gentleman*.

The **simple predicate** (verb) of a sentence is the fundamental part of the complete predicate—the verb(s) that are in the complete predicate. In the example, the simple predicate is *walked*.

A sentence may also have compound subjects and predicates.

▶ The aged, white-haired gentleman and his wife walked slowly down the hallway.

(compound subject: *gentleman* and *wife*)

▶ The aged, white-haired gentleman walked slowly and deliberately down the hallway and then paused to speak to me.

(compound verb: *walked* and *paused*)

If you have trouble locating the subject of a sentence, find the verb and then ask *who* or *what* did the verb. Read this sentence:

▶ After a tiring morning at the gym, the six young athletes fell onto the floor in exhaustion.

The verb is *fell*. If you ask, "Who or what fell?" you answer *athletes,* which is the subject.

Keep in mind that the subject of a sentence is never in a prepositional phrase. Also, if the sentence is a question, the subject sometimes appears after the verb. To find the subject, turn the question around so that it resembles a declarative sentence:

▶ What is Amy going to do with that leftover sandwich?

Now, turn the wording around so that you have:

▶ Amy is going to do what with that leftover sandwich?

Amy answers the *who?* or *what?* question about the verb *is going*.

Complements

Although some sentences are complete with only a subject and a predicate, many others need something else to complete their meaning. These additional parts of a sentence are called **complements**, and there are five types: direct object, object complement, indirect object, predicate adjective, and predicate nominative. Predicate adjectives and predicate nominatives are considered subject complements.

Direct Objects

One type of complement that is used with a transitive verb is a **direct object**: the word or words that receive the action of the verb. Direct objects are nouns (usually), pronouns (sometimes), or noun clauses (rarely). You can find the direct object by applying this formula:

1. First, find the subject of the sentence.
2. Second, find the transitive verb.
3. Third, say the subject and predicate, and then ask *whom?* or *what?* If a word answers either of those questions, it is a direct object.

All of this sounds more complicated than it is. Take a look at this sentence:

▶ The little boy constantly dribbled the basketball in the outdoor playground.

You can find the subject *(boy)* and the verb *(dribbled)*, so all you do is say *boy dribbled whom or what?* The word that answers that question *(basketball)* is the direct object. Easy enough, huh?

Mixing Things Up

In order to keep their paragraphs from being too monotonous, good writers often change the word order of their sentences from the normal subject-verb pattern. Read these two sentences:

▶ The soldiers came over the hill, determined to destroy the fortress
▶ Over the hill came the soldiers, determined to destroy the fortress.

In both sentences, the subject (*soldiers*) and the verb (*came*) are the same, but the second sentence is written in what is called inverted order—the verb comes before the subject. The caution here is to be sure that the subject agrees with the verb, no matter what order the sentence is written in.

Object Complements

Another kind of complement used with a transitive verb is an **object complement** (sometimes called an objective complement); it elaborates on or gives a fuller meaning to a direct object. Object complements can be nouns or adjectives. Take a look at this sentence:

▶ Karen asked her friend Paulette for a ride home.

In this sentence the direct object is *Paulette* (Karen asked whom or what? *Paulette*), and the noun *friend* is the object complement (it helps to complete the information about the word *Paulette*). Object complements that act in this way—that is, they elaborate on the direct object—are nouns or pronouns.

Object complements can also be adjectives. Look at this sentence:

▶ On a whim, Matthew painted his fingernails blue.

The direct object is *fingernails* (Matthew painted whom or what? *fingernails*), and the adjective *blue* is the object complement (it elaborates on the word *fingernails*). Object complements that act in this way—that is, they describe the direct object—are adjectives.

Indirect Objects

The third type of complement used with a transitive verb is an **indirect object**. It comes before a direct object and answers the question *to whom?* or *for whom?* after the subject and verb. Here is a formula for finding an indirect object:

1. First, find the subject of the sentence.
2. Second, find the transitive verb.
3. Third, say the subject and the predicate, and then ask *to whom?* or *for whom?* If a word answers that question, it is an indirect object.

Look at this example:
▶ Kyle reluctantly gave Linda the keys to his new car.

In this sentence, the subject is *Kyle* and the verb is *gave*. Using the formula of asking *to whom?* or *for whom?* after the subject and verb, you would say *Kyle gave to whom?* The answer is *Linda*.

Note: with an indirect object, the word *to* or *for* is only implied. If one of those words is actually used, a prepositional phrase is formed, not an indirect object.

▶ Kyle reluctantly gave the keys to Linda.

(*to Linda* is a prepositional phrase, and *Linda* is not an indirect object)

Subject Complements

Other kinds of complements, called **subject complements,** are used with linking verbs only. (Linking verbs, you'll remember, are all forms of *be* and, in certain situations, *appear, become, feel, grow, look, remain, smell, sound, stay,* and *taste.*) Subject complements complete (give you more information about) the subject. There are two types of subject complements: predicate adjectives and predicate nominatives.

Predicate Adjectives

A **predicate adjective** is an adjective that comes after a linking verb and describes the subject of the sentence. To find a predicate adjective, apply this formula:

1. First, make sure the sentence has a linking verb.
2. Second, find the subject of the sentence.
3. Third, say the subject, say the linking verb, and then ask *what?* If the word that answers the question *what?* is an adjective, then you have a predicate adjective.

Here is an example of a predicate adjective:
  ▶ Crystal is certainly intelligent.

Apply the formula for this sentence: (1) you know that *is* is a linking verb; (2) you find *Crystal* as the subject of the sentence; (3) you say *Crystal is what?* Since *intelligent* answers that question, and *intelligent* is an adjective (it describes the noun *Crystal*), then you know that *intelligent* is a predicate adjective.

Predicate Nominatives

The other type of subject complement is the **predicate nominative** (sometimes called the predicate noun). It also comes after a linking verb and gives you more information about the subject. A predicate nominative must be a noun or pronoun. Here's the formula for finding a predicate nominative:

1. First, make sure the sentence has a linking verb.
2. Second, find the subject of the sentence.

3.   Third, say the subject, say the linking verb, and then ask *who?*
     If the word that answers the question *who?* is a noun or pro-
     noun, you have a predicate nominative.

Look at this sentence:
▶ That man over there is DeShawn.

Apply the formula for this sentence: (1) you know that *is* is a
linking verb; (2) you find *man* as the subject of the sentence; (3) you
say *man is who?* Since *DeShawn* answers that question, and
DeShawn is a noun (it names a person), then you know that
DeShawn is a predicate nominative.

Phrases

A **phrase** is a group of words that acts as a particular part of speech or
part of a sentence but doesn't have a verb and its subject. The most
common type of phrase is the prepositional phrase.

A **prepositional phrase** is a group of words that begins with a
preposition and ends with a noun or pronoun (the object of the
preposition). Here are a few examples:
▶ during the terrible storm   ▶ for me
▶ after our dinner   ▶ with his son

In a sentence, prepositional phrases act as adjectives (that is, they
describe nouns or pronouns; they also answer the question *which
one?* or *what kind of?*) or adverbs (that is, they describe verbs, adjectives, or other adverbs; they also answer the question *when? where?
how? why? to what extent?* or *under what condition?*).

▶ **Adjective phrase:** Several friends from my job are getting
together tonight.

(*from my job* modifies or describes the noun *friends*)

▶ **Adverb phrase:** We'll meet at the restaurant at 8 P.M.

(*at the restaurant* modifies or describes the verb *meet*)

Other phrases are formed by combining a participle with related words to describe a noun or pronoun. (See Chapter 4 for a discussion of participles.) These phrases include:

▶ **Participial phrase:** Fleeing from the sudden storm, many picnickers sought refuge in the shelter house at the park.

(*Fleeing* is a present participle describing the noun *picnickers; fleeing from the sudden storm* makes up a participial phrase.)

▶ **Gerund phrase:** Singing the night away helped Joseph forget his troubles.

(*Singing* is a gerund; in this sentence, it acts as the subject. *Singing the night away* makes up a gerund phrase.)

▶ **Infinitive phrase:** "To go home is my only wish right now," sighed the tired mother after a long day of shopping with the children.

(*To go* is an infinitive; in this sentence, it acts as the subject. *To go home* makes up an infinitive phrase.)

A final type of phrase is an **appositive phrase**. An appositive is a noun (usually) or pronoun (rarely) that gives details or identifies another noun or pronoun. Here is an example:

▶ My favorite book, a dog-eared copy of *To Kill a Mockingbird*, has accompanied me on many vacations.

Copy is an appositive that refers to *book*. In this sentence, *copy* and the words that go with it—*a dog-eared*—make up the appositive phrase: *a dog-eared copy of* To Kill a Mockingbird.

Clauses

Like a phrase, a **clause** is used as a particular part of speech or part of a sentence; however, unlike a phrase, a clause has a verb and its subject.

Independent Clauses

An **independent clause** (sometimes called a main clause) is a group of words that has a verb and its subject. These words could stand alone as a sentence; that is, the words could make sense if they were by themselves. Here is an example:

▶ The white index cards fell to the floor.

This is one independent clause. It has a subject *(cards)* and a verb *(fell)*, and it stands alone as a sentence. Now, look at this sentence:

▶ The cards scattered on the floor, and I had to pick them all up.

This is made up of two independent clauses. The first—*the cards scattered on the floor*—has a subject *(cards)* and a verb *(scattered)*; it could stand alone as a sentence. The second—*I had to pick them all up*—has a subject *(I)* and a verb *(had)*; it also could stand alone as a sentence.

Subordinate Clauses

A **subordinate clause** (sometimes called a dependent clause) has a verb and its subject, but it can't stand alone as a sentence. In order for a subordinate clause to make sense, it has to be attached to another part (to some independent clause) of the sentence. Look at this example:

▶ I had just alphabetized the cards when they fell on the floor and scattered everywhere.

In this sentence, *when they fell on the floor and scattered everywhere* is a subordinate clause. It has a subject *they* and verbs *fell* and *scattered*. But read the words alone:

▶ When they fell on the floor and scattered everywhere

So, what about them? What happened next? If the terminology seems complicated, think of the relationship this way: since a subordinate clause can't stand alone, it's secondary (subordinate) to the main clause of the sentence. Or, a subordinate clause relies (is dependent) on another clause (an independent clause) that's in the sentence.

There are three types of subordinate clauses, and each acts in a different way in the sentence.

1. An **adjective clause** is a subordinate clause that acts as an adjective; it modifies or describes a noun or pronoun. It is sometimes called a relative clause because it often begins with a relative pronoun *(who, whose, whom, which,* and *that).*

▶ That man, whom I went to high school with, walked right by as if he'd never met me.

(Whom I went to high school with is an adjective clause describing the word *man.)*

Careful! Just to confuse you, sometimes an adjective clause has *that* deleted from it.

▶ The new CD that I want has not yet been released.

▶ The new CD I want has not yet been released.

2. A **noun clause** is a subordinate clause that acts as a noun; it can be the subject, predicate nominative, appositive, object of a verb, or object of a preposition.

▶ Rocky couldn't believe what he heard at the water fountain.

(What he heard at the water fountain is a noun clause serving as the direct object of *he heard.)*

3. An **adverb clause** is a subordinate clause that acts as an adverb; it can modify or describe a verb, an adjective, or another adverb. An adverb clause is introduced by a subordinating conjunction, such as *after, although, as (if), because, once, until,* and *while.*

▶ Mr. Sylvester came to visit because he needed some company for the evening.

(Because he needed some company for the evening is an adverb clause that modifies the verb *came.)*

Remember to use a comma after an introductory adverb clause, as in this example:

▶ Whenever he came to visit, Mr. Sylvester always brought a box of candy for us.

Restrictive and Nonrestrictive Clauses

Clauses are also divided in another way. A **restrictive clause** (also called an essential or defining clause) is necessary to the basic meaning of the sentence; a **nonrestrictive clause** (also called a nonessential or nondefining clause) can be eliminated from the sentence without changing its basic meaning.

▶ The car that I was driving was stolen.

▶ The car, which was stolen last Saturday, has been found.

In the first example, the clause *that I was driving* is necessary to complete the meaning of the sentence. In the second example, including the clause w*hich was stolen last Saturday* is not necessary in order to understand what the sentence says. In this instance, the clause is merely extra information.

Notice in the preceding examples that *that* is used to introduce restrictive clauses, while *which* is used to introduce nonrestrictive clauses.

Sentence Functions

Sentences function in four different ways; they can be declarative, interrogative, imperative, and exclamatory.

1. A **declarative sentence** makes a statement:

▶ I'll be seeing you tomorrow, and we can talk about our weekend plans.

2. An **interrogative sentence** asks a question:

▶ Do you think we can talk about our weekend plans tomorrow?

3. An **imperative sentence** issues a command, makes a request, or gives instructions:

▶ Come here so we can talk about our plans.

Note that in imperative sentences the actual subject of the sentence is often an unstated, but understood *you:*

▶ (You) come here so we can talk about our plans.

4. An **exclamatory sentence** expresses strong emotion:

▶ How I hope we can be together this weekend!

Subject-Verb Agreement: Keeping the Harmony

When you read your sentences, do you hear a jarring ring that tells you that something's wrong? The problem may be that you have disagreement between subjects and verbs. To smooth out the situation, you must make verbs agree with their subjects in number and in person. The first part of this rule *(make the verb agree with its subject in number)* seems simple: If you use a singular subject, you have to use a singular verb; if you use a plural subject, you have to use a plural verb. However, a number of situations can arise to make the rule tricky to follow.

The Problem of Prepositions

One problem comes from incorrectly making the verb agree with a word that is not the subject. To avoid this mistake, mentally disregard any prepositional phrases that come after the subject. Take a look at this sentence:

▶ The tray of ice cubes (**has, have**) fallen on the kitchen floor.

Since you know to disregard the prepositional phrase *of ice cubes,* you then have:

▶ The tray ~~of ice cubes~~ (**has, have**) fallen on the kitchen floor.

Now, you're left with the subject of the sentence *(tray).* Of course, you would say,

▶ "The tray has fallen on the kitchen floor."

Finding the Pronouns

When an indefinite pronoun is the subject of your sentence, you have to look at the individual pronoun. Sometimes this is a snap, as with the plural pronouns that take a plural verb *(both, few, many, others, several)*. Look at these sentences:

▶ "Several scouts are [not **is**] in the stands at tonight's game," whispered the coach.

▶ A few of us want [not **wants**] to go camping this weekend.

Just as some plural indefinite pronouns are easy to spot, so are some singular indefinite pronouns *(another, anybody, anyone, anything, each, either, everybody, everyone, everything, much, neither, no one, nobody, nothing, one, other, somebody, someone, something)*. The problem with indefinite pronouns is that a few of them are considered to be singular, even though they indicate a plural number (e.g., *each, everybody, everyone, everything*). For example:

▶ Everybody is [not **are**] here, so we can get started on the trip.

▶ No one is [not **are**] going to complain if you want to pick up the tab for tonight's meal.

Now comes a tricky rule: Five pronouns *(all, any, most, none, and some)* sometimes take a singular verb and sometimes take a plural verb. How do you know which one to use? This is the time—the only time—you break the rule about disregarding the prepositional phrases. Take a look at these sentences:

▶ "Some of the money is [not **are**] missing!" cried the teller.

▶ "Some of the people in the bank are [not **is**] the suspects," replied the policeman.

▶ Most of my coworkers are [not **is**] cleared of any suspicion.

▶ Most of my jewelry is [not **are**] still missing.

In each case, you have to look at the object of the preposition *(money, people, coworkers, jewelry)* to decide whether to use a singular or plural verb.

Special Agreement Situations

Here are some more oddities of English grammar (as if you haven't seen enough of them already):

1. The phrase *the only one of those* uses a singular verb; however, the phrase *one of those* uses a plural verb. (Is your head spinning?) Maybe these examples will help:

▶ The only one of those people I feel comfortable with is [not **are**] Gail Prince.

▶ Gail is one of those people who always listen [not **listens**] when I have a problem.

2. If you have a sentence with *every* or *many a* before a word or group of words, then use a singular verb. For example:

▶ Many a good man is [not **are**] trying to please his wife.

▶ Every wife tries [not **try**] to help her husband understand.

3. When the phrase *the number* is part of the subject of a sentence, it takes a singular verb. When the phrase *a number* is part of the subject, it takes a plural verb. Look at these sentences:

▶ The number of people who came to the concert is [not **are**] disappointing.

▶ A number of people are [not **is**] at home watching the finals of the basketball tournament.

4. When the phrase *more than one* is part of the subject, it takes a singular verb:

▶ More than one person is [not **are**] upset about the outcome of the election.

5. Another time that subjects may be singular or plural is with collective nouns. Collective nouns name groups, such as *cast, fleet,*

or *gang*. Use a singular verb if you mean that the individual members of the group act or think together (they act as one unit). Use a plural verb if you mean that the individual members of the group act or think separately. For example:

▶ The couple is renewing its yearly donation of $50,000 for scholarships.

(The two people were donating as a unit.)

▶ The couple were cleared of the charges of embezzlement of $50,000.

(The two were cleared separately.)

6. Still another problem with singular and plural verbs comes with expressions of amount. When the particular measurement or quantity (e.g., of time, money, weight, volume, food, or fractions) is considered as one unit or group, then use a singular verb:

▶ Ten dollars to see this movie is [not **are**] highway robbery!

▶ I would estimate that two thirds of the snow has [not **have**] melted.

7. Some nouns look plural but actually name one person, place, or thing, and so they are singular:

▶ The United States is [not **are**] defending its title against the United Kingdom.

(Although there are fifty states in the United States, it is only one country.)

▶ Because I think the subject is fascinating, I think it's odd that economics is [not **are**] called "the dismal science."

(*Economics* looks like a plural word, but it's only one subject.)

8. Here's another special situation: When you use the words *pants, trousers, shears, spectacles, glasses, tongs,* and *scissors* alone, you use a plural verb:

▶ These pants are [not **is**] too tight since I returned home from the cruise.

▶ Do [not **Does**] these trousers come in any other color?

But put the words *a pair of* in front of *pants, trousers, shears, spectacles, glasses, tongs,* or *scissors,* and then you need a singular verb:

▶ This pair of pants is [not **are**] too tight since I returned home from the cruise.

▶ Does [not **Do**] this pair of trousers come in any other color?

If you think about it, the logic behind the usage is strange since *pair* means *two,* and *two* denotes a plural. Oh, well . . .

Using Compound Subjects

The first rule in this part is easy. **Compound subjects** (subjects joined by *and*) take a plural verb:

▶ Mary and Mark are [not **is**] here.

▶ Mr. and Mrs. Claxton are [not **is**] joining us for an informal dinner tonight.

Here's an exception: If you have two or more subjects joined by *and*—and the subjects are thought of as one unit—then use a singular verb.

▶ Peanut butter and jelly is my favorite kind of sandwich.

The second rule is *almost* as easy. Singular subjects joined by *or* or *nor* take a singular verb:

▶ My teacher or my adviser is [not **are**] here to help me pick my new classes.

▶ The butcher, the baker, or the candlestick maker is [not **are**] coming to tomorrow's career fair.

Rule number three is along the same lines as rule number two. Plural subjects joined by *or* or *nor* take a plural verb:

▶ The Smiths or the Joneses are [not **is**] visiting tonight.

▶ The horses or the pigs are [not **is**] making too much noise tonight.

With the second and third rules, you have to be sure that the subjects joined by *or* or *nor* are either *all* singular or *all* plural. Follow these two rules:

1. If all the subjects are singular, use a singular verb.
2. If all the subjects are plural, use a plural verb.

What if you have one singular subject and one plural subject joined by *or* or *nor*? Do you use a singular or plural verb? Simple: You go by the subject that's closer to the verb. So you would write:

▶ My cat or my three dogs are [not **is**, since **dogs** is plural and is closer to the verb] coming with me on the trip.

Or, if you inverted the subjects, you would write:

▶ My three dogs or my cat is [not **are**, since **cat** is singular and is closer to the verb] making me itch all the time.

Here, There, and Everywhere

Sometimes writers and speakers have a hard time with sentences that begin with *here* or *there*.

▶ Here's the money I owe you.

or

▶ There's plenty of time left.

Writing either is fine because if you changed the contractions into the two words each represents, you'd have "Here is the money I owe you" and "There is plenty of time left."

No problem, huh? Now look at these sentences:

▶ Here's the books I told you I'd bring to you.
▶ There's lots of sandwiches left, so help yourself.

In these examples if you change those contractions, you have "Here is the books I told you I'd bring to you" and "There is lots of sandwiches left, so help yourself." Obviously, you'd never say either of those (right?), so the verb form is wrong. Since each of those subjects is plural, you need the plural verb *(are)*.

So the rule is this: If you begin a sentence with *here* or *there* and you have a plural subject, be sure to use a plural verb (usually the verb *are*).

Mixed Numbers

If you have a sentence with a plural subject and a singular predicate nominative (or vice versa), use the verb that agrees with the subject, not the predicate nominative. For example:

▶ Although they're very expensive, Susie's favorite present is pink roses.

▶ Although they're very expensive, pink roses are Susie's favorite present.

In the first sentence the subject *(present)* is singular, so the singular verb *(is)* is used. In the second sentence the subject *(roses)* is plural, so the plural verb *(are)* is used.

Chapter 4

Verb Varieties

One might say that "a rose is a rose is a rose" (or "a noun is a noun is a noun"), but verbs are not so simple. Even a garden-variety verb, such as *grow,* can go back to the past *(grew),* leap to the future *(will grow),* and change in number *(it grows, they grow).* It can even transform itself into a verbal *(growing, grown,* or *to grow).* With all of this variety, is it surprising that the verb is the part of speech that has several different moods?

In this chapter, we'll sort out all these forms. When we're done, choosing the right verb will never again make you tense.

Verbals

Besides eight main parts of speech, there are three other parts—participles, gerunds, and infinitives—called **verbals**. Verbals are hybrids that don't act as verbs in a sentence, but as other parts of speech.

Participles

A **participle** is part verb and part something else, but it's used as an adjective. (Remember that adjectives answer one of three questions: *which one? what kind of?* or *how many?*) Some participles consist of a verb plus *–ing*, as in these sentences:

▶ Just let sleeping dogs lie.

Sleeping consists of the verb *sleep* plus the ending *–ing*, and it acts as an adjective in the sentence. It describes *dogs*, and it answers the question *which ones?*

▶ Shivering from the cold, Robert went immediately to the coffeepot and poured himself a large cup.

Shivering consists of the verb *shiver* plus the ending *–ing*, and it acts as an adjective in the sentence. It describes *Robert*, and it answers the question *what kind of?* or *which one?*

These are examples of **present participles**.

Other participles, called **past participles**, consist of a verb plus *–d* or *–ed*, as in these sentences:

▶ The entire team, exhilarated from the unexpected victory, embraced the cheering fans.

Exhilarated consists of the verb *exhilarate* plus the ending *–ed*, and it acts as an adjective in the sentence. It describes *team*, and it answers the question *what kind of?*

So what's the big deal about a participle? Sometimes it's used in the wrong way, and that creates a **dangling participle** (also called a hanging participle or an unattached participle). Take a look at this sentence:

▶ Babbling incoherently, the nurse quickly wrapped his arms around the child.

The way the sentence is written, it seems that the nurse was babbling (a participle) incoherently. What the writer means (at least, what we hope he or she means) is that the child was babbling incoherently. The sentence should be rewritten, perhaps this way:

▶ The nurse quickly wrapped his arms around the babbling child.

Gerunds

Like a present participle, a **gerund** is a word that begins with a verb and ends in –*ing*. Unlike a participle, though, a gerund acts like a noun (that is, it names a person, place, or thing) in a sentence.

▶ Running up steep hills for the last six months has greatly increased my stamina.

▶ Hector thought he could impress his boss by staying late at the office.

Running is a gerund. It is composed of a verb *(run)*, ends in –*ing*, and is used as a noun in the sentence. *Staying* is another gerund. It is composed of a verb *(stay)*, ends in –*ing*, and is used as a noun in the sentence.

Here's a rule that is often ignored: Use a possessive noun or possessive pronoun *(my, your, his, her, its, our,* and *their)* before a gerund. Look at this sentence:

▶ James continues to be amazed by (Barbara, Barbara's) singing.

You would use the possessive *Barbara's* before the gerund *singing.* The same is true for this sentence:

▶ I was upset about (us, our) leaving so early in the morning.

The possessive pronoun *our* should be used before the gerund *leaving.*

Infinitives

An **infinitive** is composed of *to* plus a verb (e.g., *to go, to carry, to drive*). Most of the time you will see infinitives used as nouns, but sometimes they crop up as adjectives or adverbs.

▶ "I want to go home!" cried the youngster.

(*To go* is an infinitive acting as a noun.)

▶ We come to bury Caesar.

(*To bury* is an infinitive that acts as an adverb; it tells why we came.)

▶ Harry was the first guy in our crowd to marry.

(*To marry* is an infinitive that acts as an adjective; it describes *guy.*)

Now for the bad news. Sometimes the *to* part of an infinitive is omitted.

▶ "Please help me make the bed before your parents get here," Arthur said to his wife.

That sentence means the same as

▶ "Please help me to make the bed . . . "

Once you get used to looking at sentences in this way, you'll find that recognizing infinitives without the *to* will become automatic.

To Split or Not to Split

Many years ago grammarians decided that it was wrong to split an infinitive (that is, to insert a word between *to* and the verb, as in *to plainly see*). For most people today, that rule is an unnecessary anachronism. For example, look at the following sentence:

▶ Georgia needed to better understand the rules of English grammar.

Wouldn't that sentence be less clear if the infinitive was not split?:

▶ Georgia needed to understand better the rules of English grammar.

or

▶ Georgia needed better to understand the rules of English grammar.

Let your ear tell you whether a split infinitive works. If it does, then by all means use it; if not, leave the infinitive alone.

Verb Tenses

English verbs are divided into three main tenses, which relate to time: **present, past,** and **future.** Each main tense is also subdivided into other categories: **simple tense, progressive tense, perfect tense,** and **perfect progressive tense.** These subcategories differentiate when a particular action has been done (or is being done or will be done).

	Simple	Progressive	Perfect	Perfect Progressive
Present	hide	am/is/are hiding	have/has hidden	have/has been hiding
Past	hid	was/were hiding	had hidden	had been hiding
Future	will/shall hide	will be hiding	will have hidden	will have been hiding

The Simple Tense: It's Elementary

The *simple present tense* tells an action that is usual or repeated:
- ▶ I hide from the Mafia.

The *simple past tense* tells an action that both began and ended in the past:
- ▶ I hid from the Mafia.

The *simple future tense* tells an upcoming action that will occur:
- ▶ I will hide from the Mafia.

The Progressive Tense: One Step Beyond

Use the *present progressive tense* to show an action that's in progress at the time the statement is written, like the following.

▶ I am hiding from the Mafia today.

Present progressive verbs are always formed by using *am*, *is*, or *are* and adding –*ing* to the verb.

Use the *past progressive tense* to show an action that was going on at some particular time in the past:

▶ I was hiding from the Mafia yesterday.

Past progressive verbs are always formed by using *was* or *were* and adding –*ing* to the verb.

Use the *future progressive tense* to show an action that's continuous and that will occur in the future:

▶ I will be hiding from the Mafia tomorrow.

Future progressive verbs are always formed by using *will be* or *shall be* and adding –*ing* to the verb.

The Perfect Tense: From the Past

The *present perfect tense* conveys action that happened sometime in the past or that started in the past but is ongoing in the present:

▶ I have hidden from the Mafia for more than five years.

Present perfect verbs are always formed by using *has* or *have* and the past participle form of the verb.

Use the *past perfect tense* to indicate past action that occurred prior to another past action:

▶ I had hidden from the Mafia for more than five years before I entered the Witness Protection Program.

Past perfect verbs are always formed by using *had* and the past participle form of the verb.

Use the *future perfect tense* to illustrate future action that will occur before some other action:

▶ I will have hidden from the Mafia for more than five years before entering the Witness Protection Program.

Future perfect verbs are always formed by using *will have* and the past participle form of the verb.

The Perfect Progressive Tense: Then, Now, and Maybe Later

Use the *present perfect progressive* to illustrate an action repeated over a period of time in the past, continuing in the present, and possibly carrying on in the future:

▶ For the past five years, I have been hiding from the Mafia.

Present perfect progressive verbs are always formed by using *has been* or *have been* and adding *–ing* to the verb.

Use the *past perfect progressive* to illustrate a past continuous action that was completed before some other past action:

▶ Before I entered the Witness Protection Program, I had been hiding from the Mafia for more than five years.

Past perfect progressive verbs are always formed by using *had been* and adding *–ing* to the verb.

Use the *future perfect progressive* to illustrate a future continuous action that will be completed before some future time:

▶ Next month I will have been hiding from the Mafia for more than five years.

Future perfect progressive verbs are always formed by using *will have been* and adding *–ing* to the verb.

Irregular Verbs

Most English verbs form their past and past participle by adding *–d* or *–ed* to the base form of the verb (the form you'd find listed first in the dictionary). These are called **regular verbs**.

Unfortunately, a number of verb forms aren't formed in that way; these are called **irregular verbs**. Here is a list of many of those troublesome verbs.

Base (Infinitive)	Simple Past	Past Participle
arise	arose	arisen
be	was, were	been
bear	bore	borne/born
become	became	become
begin	began	begun
bend	bent	bent
bet	bet/betted	bet/betted
bid	bade/bid	bidden/bid
bind	bound	bound
bite	bit	bitten/bit
bleed	bled	bled
blow	blew	blown
break	broke	broken
bring	brought	brought
build	built	built
burn	burned/burnt	burned/burnt
burst	burst	burst
buy	bought	bought
catch	caught	caught
choose	chose	chosen
come	came	come
creep	crept	crept
cut	cut	cut
deal	dealt	dealt
dive	dived/dove	dived
do	did	done
draw	drew	drawn
dream	dreamed/dreamt	dreamed/dreamt
drink	drank	drunk
drive	drove	driven
eat	ate	eaten

Base (Infinitive)	Simple Past	Past Participle
fall	fell	fallen
feed	fed	fed
feel	felt	felt
find	found	found
fit	fitted/fit	fit
fly	flew	flown
freeze	froze	frozen
get	got	gotten/got
give	gave	given
go	went	gone
grow	grew	grown
hang (to suspend)	hung	hung
has	had	had
have	had	had
hear	heard	heard
hide	hid	hidden/hid
hit	hit	hit
hold	held	held
keep	kept	kept
know	knew	known
lay	laid	laid
lead	led	led
leap	leaped/leapt	leaped/leapt
learn	learned/learnt	learned/learnt
leave	left	left
lie (to rest or recline)	lay	lain
light	lighted/lit	lighted/lit
lose	lost	lost
make	made	made
mean	meant	meant
meet	met	met

Base (Infinitive)	Simple Past	Past Participle
mistake	mistook	mistaken
mow	mowed	mowed/mown
pay	paid	paid
plead	pleaded/pled	pleaded/pled
prove	proved/proven	proved/proven
quit	quit/quitted	quit/quitted
ride	rode	ridden
ring	rang	rung
rise	rose	risen
run	ran	run
saw (to cut)	sawed	sawed/sawn
say	said	said
see	saw	seen
sell	sold	sold
send	sent	sent
set	set	set
sew	sewed	sewn/sewed
shake	shook	shaken
shine	shone/shined	shone/shined
show	showed	shown/showed
shrink	shrank/shrunk	shrunk/shrunken
shut	shut	shut
sing	sang/sung	sung
sink	sank/sunk	sunk
sit	sat	sat
sleep	slept	slept
slide	slid	slid
sling	slung	slung
smell	smelled/smelt	smelled/smelt
speak	spoke	spoken
speed	sped/speeded	sped/speeded

Base (Infinitive)	Simple Past	Past Participle
spell	spelled/spelt	spelled/spelt
spend	spent	spent
spill	spilled/spilt	spilled/spilt
spin	spun	spun
spoil	spoiled/spoilt	spoiled/spoilt
spring	sprang/sprung	sprung
steal	stole	stolen
stick	stuck	stuck
sting	stung	stung
stink	stank/stunk	stunk
strike	struck	struck/stricken
string	strung	strung
swear	swore	sworn
sweep	swept	swept
swim	swam	swum
swing	swung	swung
take	took	taken
teach	taught	taught
tear	tore	torn
tell	told	told
think	thought	thought
throw	threw	thrown
wake	woke/waked	waked/woken
wear	wore	worn
weave	wove	woven
weep	wept	wept
wet	wet/wetted	wet/wetted
win	won	won
wind	wound	wound

Moods

English verbs are divided into **moods**, which show the writer's attitude toward what he or she is saying.

Almost all verbs are used in the **indicative mood**, which means that the verb's sentence states an actuality. Some examples:

▶ I'll be seeing you later on tonight. We'll go to the movies with our friends. You may wear whatever you want.

The **imperative mood** is used to make requests or give commands. For example:

▶ Please give me the phone.

▶ Give it to me—or else!

The **subjunctive mood** is used with only two verbs *(be* and *were)* and in only two kinds of sentences:

1. Statements that are contrary to fact (providing they begin with *if* or *unless*), improbable, or doubtful; and

2. Statements that express a wish, a request or recommendation, an urgent appeal, or a demand

The following are verb forms used in the subjunctive mood:

Present Subjunctive		**Past Subjunctive**	
Singular	*Plural*	*Singular*	*Plural*
(if) I be	(if) we be	(if) I were	(if) we were
(if) he/she/it be	(if) they be	(if) you were	(if) you were
(if) you be	(if) you be	(if) he/she/it were	(if) they were

Here are several examples:

▶ Mary Alice moved that the minutes be [not **are**] accepted. (expresses a request)

▶ If I were [not **was**] a millionaire, I would buy you a car. (contrary to fact)

▶ It's important that everybody be [not **is**] at the meeting early. (wish or request)

Chapter 5

Pronoun Problems

Perhaps pronouns—if they only knew—would be proud that they are the only part of speech besides verbs judged worthy of their own chapter in *The Only Grammar Book You'll Ever Need*. Unfortunately, it's not meant as a compliment. Handy and timesaving as they are, pronouns frequently pose problems for both speakers and writers. (Unlike, for example, those cheerful interjections that almost never—thank goodness!—cause any grammatical trouble.) Yet using the proper pronoun is essential to avoid both confusion and miscommunication.

In this chapter, we'll settle some disagreements, find the right persons, clear up some vague references, and solve some puzzling cases. We'll even master that age-old "who-whom" problem. By the end, you'll be able to use pronouns—even those tricky indefinite ones—confidently and correctly.

First, a quick reminder: Pronouns are words that take the place of nouns. They include the following.

all	herself	nobody	themselves
another	him	none	these
any	himself	nothing	they
anybody	his	one	this
anyone	I	other	those
anything	it	others	us
both	itself	ours	what
each	little	ourselves	which
either	many	several	who
everybody	me	she	whom
everyone	mine	some	whose
everything	most	somebody	you
few	much	someone	yours
he	myself	that	yourself
her	neither	theirs	yourselves
hers	no one	them	

Problems with Agreement

Pronouns must agree in number with the words they refer to (their antecedents). Read this sentence:

> ► After I saw whom the letters were from, I tossed it in the wastebasket.

The sentence doesn't make sense because *it* is the wrong pronoun. *Letters* is a plural noun, so the pronoun used to replace it should also be plural. To correct the sentence, *it* must be replaced by the plural pronoun *them*.

Put another way, the rule is this: If a pronoun is plural, the word it refers to (also known as its antecedent) must be plural; if a pronoun is singular, the word it refers to must be singular.

Problems with Indefinite Pronouns

Indefinite pronouns include the following:

all	either	much	others
another	everybody	neither	several
any	everyone	no one	some
anybody	everything	nobody	somebody
anyone	few	none	someone
anything	little	nothing	something
both	many	one	
each	most	other	

Anyone, anybody, anything, each, either, everybody, everyone, everything, neither, nobody, none, no one, one, somebody, something, and *someone* are all considered to be singular words, so they all require a singular pronoun. But, if you think about it, the word *each* (for instance) implies more than one. If each person is doing something, that means more than one, right? The same can be said for *everybody, everything,* and *everyone.* This doesn't matter; all four words are considered singular. So you should write:

▶ Everybody is seated, and each is waiting for the plane to take off.

▶ Each of the dogs needs its personalized collar before it can be enrolled in dog obedience school.

A common tendency in everyday speech is to use *they* or *their* in place of some singular pronouns. In the first example, you might hear the sentence spoken this way:

▶ Everybody is seated, and they are waiting for the plane to take off.

This usage is called the "singular they" because *they* refers to an antecedent that's singular.

An Exception to the Rule

Remember the rule that says to disregard any prepositional phrase when you're looking for the subject of a sentence? Take a look at these two sentences:

▶ All of the money is missing from the safe.

▶ All of the cookies are missing from the jar.

In both sentences, the subject is *all*. But the first sentence has a singular verb and the second sentence has a plural verb—and both are correct.

With five pronouns (*all, any, most, none,* and *some*), the "disregard the prepositional phrase" rule doesn't apply. For those five pronouns, look at the object of the preposition to determine which verb to use.

Even though using the "singular they" is becoming more commonplace, its usage is still frowned on in some circles. However, this may be one of the rules of grammar that eventually changes, as using the "singular they" helps prevent an overuse of *his or her* or *he or she.* For example, consider the following paragraph:

▶ When I came downstairs, everybody in the family was already eating their breakfast, and everyone was engrossed in reading their different sections of the newspaper. Each of them seemed to be in their own little world.

By changing the pronouns to agree in number with their antecedents, you would have:

▶ When I came downstairs, everybody in the family was already eating *his or her* breakfast, and everyone was engrossed in reading *his or her* different sections of the newspaper. Each of them seemed to be in *his or her* own little world.

While the second version may be grammatically correct, it sure doesn't read well. One way to avoid this awkwardness is to rewrite the sentences to use plural nouns and pronouns instead of singular ones:

▶ When I came downstairs, all of my family members were

already eating their breakfast. All of them were engrossed in reading their own sections of the newspaper. They seemed to be in their own little world.

Much better, isn't it?

Vague Pronoun References

As you recall, pronouns are words that take the place of nouns; antecedents are the nouns that the pronouns refer to. For example:

▶ Shirley called to say she would be glad to help decorate for the party on Friday.

In this example, the pronoun *she* clearly refers to a specific noun *Shirley* (its antecedent). But take a look at this sentence:

▶ Billy Joe invited Darrell to the ranch because he enjoyed horseback riding.

Well, now. Just whom does the word *he* in the second part of the sentence refer to—Billy Joe or Darrell? The antecedent of *he* isn't clear.

To make the sentence read clearly, it should be reworded:

▶ Because Darrell enjoyed horseback riding, Billy Joe invited him to the ranch.

or

▶ Billy Joe, who enjoyed horseback riding, invited Darrell to the ranch.

Sometimes a pronoun has no reference at all. Read this sentence:

▶ Karen was afraid he would not remember to pick up the refreshments for the party.

Just who is *he*? Unless the man has been identified in an earlier sentence, the reader is left out in the cold about his identity.

Remember that an antecedent has to refer to a specific person, place, or thing. Look at the following sentence.

▶ The young recording star was elated, but he kept it hidden.

What did the star keep hidden? Was *it* supposed to refer to the fact that he felt elated? In that case, the sentence would read:

▶ The young recording star was elated, but he kept elated hidden.

Doesn't make sense, does it? The word *elated* can't be the antecedent of *it* because *elated* isn't a person, place, or thing. The sentence needs to be reworded something like this:

▶ The young recording star was elated with his hit record, but he kept his feelings hidden.

Along the same lines, sometimes in a sentence there is a noun that the pronoun refers to, but it's not the right noun; the correct reference is missing from the sentence. Read this sentence:

▶ After a successful fishing trip with his brothers, Steve let them all go.

The way the sentence is now worded, Steve let his brothers go. That's what *them* refers to in the sentence. What the writer actually means is that Steve let all the fish go. The sentence should be rewritten like this:

▶ After a successful fishing trip with his brothers, Steve let all of their catch go.

Here's another example of a pronoun that doesn't refer to the right antecedent:

▶ The new tax forms arrived today. They want me to fill out every line on the last three pages.

The way this sentence is worded, the tax forms want you to do the filling out. What the writer meant was that the Internal Revenue Service, or an accounting firm, or the office personnel at work—someone the writer had failed to name—wants the tax forms filled out. The sentence needs to be reworded to make it clear who *they* are.

▶ The new tax forms arrived today. Our accountant wants me to fill out every line on the last three pages.

Be careful not to use *they* when you refer to unnamed persons; said another way, *they* must refer to people you specify. The same holds true for any pronoun, but *they, he, she,* and *it* are the ones most commonly misused in this way. If you think that you may have an unclear reference, one way to test the sentence is to do this:

1. Find the pronoun.
2. Replace the pronoun with its antecedent—the noun it refers to (remember, the noun must be the exact word).
3. If the sentence doesn't make sense, you need to reword your sentence.

Choosing the Right Person

You may have instructions that call for your piece of writing to be written in a particular person—first person, second person, or third person.

First-person pronouns include *I, me, my, mine, we, our,* and *us,* and the first-person point of view expresses the personal point of view of the speaker or author *(I will bring the book to Jack).* **Second-person pronouns** include *you, your,* and *yours,* and material expressed in the second-person point of view directly addresses the listener or reader *(You will bring the book to Jack).* **Third-person pronouns** include *he, she, him, her, his, hers, they, them, their,* and *theirs.* In the third-person point of view, material is expressed from the point of view of a detached writer or other characters *(They will bring the book to Jack).*

If you're writing for a class, be sure to check with the instructor to determine if there is a requirement about using first, second, or third person. (Most academic writing must be in the third person.) If you're writing for a company, check to see if there are particular guidelines about which person you should use. (If you're still in doubt, use third person.)

Shifts in Person

One of the most common problems in writing comes with a shift in person. The writer begins in either first or third person and then—without reason—shifts to second person. Take, for example, this paragraph:

▶ Even in a casual atmosphere I can be embarrassed by someone else, and this causes you to become tense. For instance, somebody you know can embarrass you at a party or in a class. It's so simple for a stranger to embarrass you. This can be upsetting, depending on the kind of person you are; it can be hurtful even if you are mentally strong.

The writer begins in the first person (telling about himself or herself by using the pronoun *I*) and then shifts to second person. The constant use of *you* sounds as if the writer is preaching directly to the reader. That writer doesn't know the reader and doesn't know if he or she can easily be embarrassed by others, and so on. Except for the beginning sentence, the entire paragraph should be rewritten and put into first person. Here is one way of doing that:

▶ Even in a casual atmosphere I can be embarrassed by someone else, and this causes me to become tense. For instance, somebody I know can embarrass me at a party or in a class. It's so simple for a stranger to embarrass me. This can be upsetting because of the kind of person I am, and it can be hurtful even if I am mentally strong.

If you begin in third person (which is the most common way of writing), stay in third person. If you begin in first person (the second most common way of writing), stay in first person. If you begin in second person, stay in second person. Consistency is the key.

Using the Second Person

Sometimes you are looking for a more informal tone than third person provides. Something written in second person (using *you* and *your*) will have a more conversational tone than writing in first or third person. Take a look at this paragraph:

▶ You'll need to watch the mixture carefully, and you may have to stir it quite often. When you get to the last step, make sure you add the final three ingredients slowly. If you add them too quickly, the combination will not blend and you'll have a mess on your hands.

That paragraph is talking directly to you, telling you what to do in your cooking. But look at the same paragraph written in third person:

▶ The mixture must be watched carefully, and it may have to be stirred quite often. At the last step, it is important that the final three ingredients be added slowly. If they are added too quickly, the combination will not blend and a mess will be created.

Now, that's pretty boring and stilted, isn't it? The directions are far better if you write them in the second person.

Pronoun Cases

Pronouns are also one of three cases: subjective, objective, and possessive. The way a pronoun is used in the sentence determines which case you should use.

1. **Subjective pronouns** include *I, you, he, she, it, we,* and *they.*
2. **Objective pronouns** include *me, you, him, her, it, us,* and *them.* (Note that *you* and *it* are included on both lists; you'll see why later.)

3. **Possessive pronouns** include *my*, *your*, *his*, *her*, *its*, *our*, and *their.* (Possessive pronouns are regarded as adjectives by some grammarians. These pronouns won't be discussed in this section because there's rarely a problem with using them correctly.)

Subjective Pronouns

Subjective pronouns are used as the subjects of sentences (whom or what you're talking about). Some examples:

▶ *I* am going to leave for my appointment.

▶ *She* is late already.

▶ *They* will never make it on time.

A problem occasionally arises when subjects are compound. You might read, for instance:

▶ His brothers and *him* are going to the ball game.

▶ Margaret, Elizabeth, and *me* were at the mall for four hours yesterday.

▶ *Me* and *her* see eye-to-eye on lots of things.

These pronouns are used incorrectly. Because the pronouns are used as subjects of the sentence, they should all be in the subjective case: *I*, *you*, *he*, *she*, *it*, *we*, or *they*. So, the sentences should read:

▶ His brothers and he are going to the ball game.

▶ Margaret, Elizabeth, and I were at the mall for four hours yesterday.

▶ I and she see eye-to-eye on lots of things.

(Actually, it's considered polite to put the other person first, so it's better to word this sentence like this: *She and I see eye-to-eye on lots of things.*)

If you're not sure if you've used the right pronoun, try writing or saying the sentence with only one subject. You'd never say:

▶ Him is going to the ball game.

or

▶ Me was at the mall for four hours yesterday.

Change the pronouns to the ones you'd normally use when there's just one subject (he and I).

Objective Pronouns

Objective pronouns are used as the objects in sentences. You would say, for instance:

▶ Terry came to see her last night.

▶ For the twins' birthday, Mother gave them several new CDs.

As with compound subjects, problems arise when there are compound objects. People sometimes write or say sentences like this:

▶ The argument arose last night between Carla and she.

▶ Please buy a raffle ticket from Nonnie or I.

Again, each pronoun is used incorrectly in these sentences. The pronouns are used as objects here and should all be in the objective case: *me, you, him, her, it, us,* and *them.* So, the sentences should read:

▶ The argument arose last night between Carla and her.

▶ Please buy a raffle ticket from Nonnie or me.

You can use the same trick that you used for the subjective pronoun problem, but substitute the objective form; that is, write or say the sentence with only one object. You'd never say:

▶ The argument arose last night between she.

▶ Please buy a raffle ticket from I.

Since those pronouns sound wrong when they're by themselves, you know that they're the wrong case. Change the pronouns to the ones you'd normally say when there is only one object.

So why were *you* and *it* on the lists of both subjective and objective pronouns? Because, unlike other pronouns on the lists (*I* and *me,* for example), English uses the same form for those two words.

▶ It was nice to get a surprise in the mail.

(*It* is used as a subject.)

▶ I got it in the mail.

(*It* is used as an object.)

▶ You called me at four o'clock?

(*You* is used as a subject.)

▶ I called you back at five o'clock.

(*You* is used as an object.)

Situations with *Than* and *As*

Another problem with pronouns sometimes arises in a sentence with words that are omitted following *than* or *as*.

Look at the following examples:

▶ Greg said to Grace, "I always thought Mother liked you more than me."

▶ Greg said to Grace, "I always thought Mother liked you more than I."

When the words that have been omitted after *than* are restored, the real meaning of the sentences becomes clear:

▶ Greg said to Grace, "I always thought Mother liked you more than (she liked) me."

▶ Greg said to Grace, "I always thought Mother liked you more than I (liked you)."

(Either way, Greg seems to be in quite a snit, doesn't he?)

The same type of confusion can result when words following *as* have been omitted. For example, someone might say or write something along the lines of:

▶ My husband finds physics as interesting as me.

This implies that, to the husband, the subject of physics and his wife are of equal interest. Now, look at the correction:

▶ My husband finds physics as interesting as I (do).

This signifies that both spouses are equally interested in physics—which, one hopes, is the intended meaning here.

By mentally adding the missing verb at the end of a sentence using *than* or *as* in this way, you'll be able to tell which pronoun to use.

Who and *Whom*: A Different Slant

Deciding whether to use *who* or *whom* may be the most difficult of all the problems with pronouns. Do you say, "The man who I called this morning has already placed an order" or "The man whom I called this morning has already placed an order"? How can you make your mind up between "The student who is early will get the best seat" and "The student whom is early will get the best seat"?

If you have trouble deciding whether to use *who* or *whom* (or *whoever* or *whomever*), try the following method.

1. First, remember to look only at the clause associated with *who* or *whom*. In some sentences, there is only one clause, and that makes finding the right word easy. Often, though, there is more than one clause (an independent clause and one or more dependent clauses).
2. Next, scramble the words of the clause (if you have to) so that the words form a statement, not a question.
3. Now, substitute either *he* or *him* for *who* or *whom*. This will tell you whether to use *who* or *whom*. Use the mnemonic *he* = *who*, *him* = *whom* (the final *m* helps you remember the association).
4. Be on the lookout for predicate nominatives. After you scramble the words, if you have a linking verb rather than an action verb, use *he (who)* instead of *him (whom)*.

Ready to put all this to a test? Try this sentence:
▶ **(Who, Whom)** telephoned so late last night?
In this sentence, no scrambling is necessary. You can substitute *he* and have a perfectly good sentence: *He telephoned so late last night*. Since you substituted *he* instead of *him* (remember that *he* =

who), you know to use *who* in the original question.

Now, try this example:

▶ **(Who**, **Whom)** were you telephoning so late at night?

Scramble the words to make a statement; then substitute *he* or *him,* and you have the statement "You were telephoning him so late at night." Since you used *him* in the new sentence, you know to use *whom* in the original question.

Now, for a trickier example:

▶ Eugene worried about **(who**, **whom)** Eddie would be teamed with in the competition.

This sentence has two clauses, but you're *only* concerned with the clause that contains the *who/whom* question. Take the words after *about,* scramble them to make a statement, substitute *he* or *him,* and you have "Eddie would be teamed with him in the competition." Since you used *him,* you would know that the original sentence would use *whom* (remember the mnemonic *him* = *whom*), like this:

▶ Eugene worried about whom Eddie would be teamed with in the competition.

Chapter 6

Punctuation and Style

When readers and writers don't use the same format—the same code—for applying capital letters and punctuation marks, confusion is often the result. Take a look at the following:

▶ when the envelope arrived i opened it and screamed this is it i yelled loudly enough to wake up the whole neighborhood running up from the basement my husband asked whats wrong nothings wrong i hastened to reply weve just become the latest winners in the state sweepstakes now well have enough money to go on that vacation weve dreamed about

Obviously, the words are jumbled together without any capitalization or punctuation. If the story is rewritten and uses appropriate capital letters and punctuation marks, then reading it becomes a snap.

▶ When the envelope arrived, I opened it and screamed. "This is it!" I yelled loudly enough to wake up the whole neighborhood.

Running up from the basement, my husband asked, "What's wrong?"

"Nothing's wrong," I hastened to reply. "We've just become the latest winners in the state sweepstakes. Now we'll have enough money to go on that vacation we've dreamed about."

Much better, wouldn't you say? The same words are used, but now you can easily read and understand the story because capital letters and punctuation marks have been correctly inserted.

Ending a Sentence

Let's begin at the end—of sentences, that is. There are three marks that signal that a sentence is over: a period, a question mark, and an exclamation point.

Periods

A **period** is most often used to signal the end of a declarative sentence (one that states a fact) or an imperative sentence (one that gives a command or states a request). For example:

▶ **Declarative sentence:** The majority of the viewers stopped watching the program after the format was changed.

▶ **Imperative sentence:** Hand me the pen that rolled near you.

Periods are also used in abbreviations: *Dr.*, *Mr.*, *Ms.*, *Rev.*, *i.e.*, *etc.*, and *et al.*

Question Marks

A **question mark** goes at the end of a direct question or a sentence that ends in questions. (You knew that, didn't you?) It is also used to show that there is doubt or uncertainty about something written in the sentence, such as a name, a date, or a word. In birth and death dates, such as (?–1565), the question mark means that the birth date has not been verified. Look at these examples:

► The police are searching for a fugitive known only as Richard-O (?) in connection with the crime.

(uncertainty about the person's name)

► Paul said he would donate five thousand (?) dollars to the charity.

(uncertainty about the exact amount of the donation)

Be sure to include question marks that are parts of titles:

► I refuse to watch that new television program *Can You Believe It?*

If you have a series of questions that are not complete sentences, a question mark should be included after each fragment:

► Can you believe that it's ten below zero? or that it's snowing? or that my electricity has gone off? or that the telephone has gone out? or that I'm completely out of snacks to get me through this weather?

Exclamation Points

An **exclamation point** (exclamation mark) is used to express strong feelings. There's quite a difference between these two sentences:

► Out of the blue, Marsha called Kyle last night.

► Out of the blue, Marsha called Kyle last night!

The second sentence tells the reader that there was something extraordinary about the fact that Marsha called Kyle.

In formal writing, don't use an exclamation point (unless, of course, you're quoting a source or citing a title with an exclamation point). In informal writing, you might include exclamation points after information that you find to be remarkable or information that you're excited about:

► Paul said that he would donate five thousand dollars (!) to the charity.

or

▶ Paul said that he would donate five thousand dollars to the charity!

As with question marks, check to see if an exclamation point is part of a title. If it is, be sure to include it:

▶ I refuse to watch that new television program *I Can't Believe It!*

Quotation Marks

The most common use of **quotation marks** ("/") is to show the reader the exact words a person said, in the exact order the person spoke them. This is called a direct quotation. Note the difference in the following sentences:

▶ **Direct quotation:** The bank robber said, "Hand over the money."

▶ **Indirect quotation:** The bank robber said to hand over the money.

The same meaning is conveyed either way, but the use of quotation marks tells the reader that the words are being stated exactly as they were spoken.

One of the most common mistakes made with quotation marks is to use them immediately after a word such as *said* or *asked* in sentences that are actually indirect quotations (that is, not the exact words, in the exact order, that the speaker used). For example:

▶ **Correct:** Harry asked if Anna would pass him the butter.

▶ **Incorrect:** Harry asked, "If Anna would pass him the butter."

Some Guidelines for Quotations

Guideline #1. Every time you change speakers, indent and make a new paragraph, even if the person quoted is just saying one word. This allows the reader to keep straight who's saying what.

Take a look at this sequence:

▶ Nick picked up the receiver and said, "Hello." A voice asked, "Who is this?" "Nick." "Nick who?" "Well, who is this?" "You know darned well who this is."

Written that way, it is difficult for the reader to follow who is saying what. The dialogue should start a new paragraph each time the speaker changes. That way, the reader can identify the speaker. This is the way the passage should be written:

▶ Nick picked up the receiver and said, "Hello."

A voice asked, "Who is this?"

"Nick."

"Nick who?"

"Well, who is this?"

"You know darned well who this is."

Guideline #2. If you're quoting more than one sentence from the same source (a person or a manuscript), put the closing quotation marks at the end of the speaker's last sentence of that paragraph *only,* not at the end of each sentence. For example:

▶ At the diner, Geoff said, "I'll start with a cup of coffee and a large orange juice. Then I want scrambled eggs, bacon, and toast for breakfast. May I get home fries with that?"

Note that there are no quotation marks after *juice* or *breakfast.* That tells the reader that Geoff hasn't finished speaking.

Guideline #3. If you're quoting more than one paragraph from the same source (a person or a manuscript), put beginning quotation marks at the start of each paragraph of your quote and closing quotation marks at the end *only*. This lets the reader know that the words come from the same source, without any interruption. Take a look at this example:

▶ The ransom letter read:

"We'll expect to receive the ransom money by this afternoon. You can get it from your Grandfather Perkins. We know he's loaded.

"Tell him not to try any funny stuff. We want the money in unmarked bills, and we don't want any police involved. We'll be in touch in ten hours to tell you where to deliver the dough. Just get it and keep your mouth shut."

Note that at the end of the first paragraph the word *loaded* doesn't have quotation marks after it, and there are quotation marks at the beginning and end of the second paragraph. This shows the reader that the same person is speaking or the same source is being quoted. The closing quotation marks designate when the quotation ends.

Guideline #4. Use quotation marks to enclose the titles of short works (short poems, short stories, titles of articles from magazines or newspapers, essays, chapters of books, songs, and episodes of television or radio programs):

▶ Harry consulted a chapter called "The Art of Detection" from the book *How Mysteries Are Written.*

▶ I particularly enjoy the song "Love Letters," which is on the CD *ABC and XYZ of Love.*

Guideline #5. If you're using slang, technical terms, or other expressions outside the normal usage, enclose them in quotation marks:

▶ My grandmother didn't know if it was a compliment or an insult when I described my best friend as being "phat."

▶ In computer discussion groups, what does "start a new thread" mean?

Guideline #6. Remember that periods and commas go *inside* closing quotation marks; colons and semicolons go *outside* closing quotation marks. This may not always look right (and it's not adhered to in British English), but that is the way it is done in the United States. Look at this sentence:

▶ I was reading the short story "Scared Out of My Wits," but I fell asleep in spite of myself.

See the comma after *Wits* and before the closing quotation marks? Now look at this sentence:

▶ I was reading the short story "Scared Out of My Wits"; I didn't find it to be scary at all.

The semicolon is *outside* the closing quotation marks after *Wits*.

Guideline #7. The two other end marks of punctuation—the question mark and the exclamation mark—go either *inside* or *outside* the closing marks, depending on what's being quoted. A question mark, for instance, goes *inside* the closing quotation if what is being quoted is a question:

▶ Martha said, "Did you fall asleep reading the story?"

The actual words that Martha said form the question, so the question mark goes *inside* the closing quotation mark. Exclamation marks are used in the same way:

▶ Martha shouted, "I hope you know what you're doing!"

Now take a look at this example:

▶ Did Martha say, "You must have fallen asleep"?

The actual words that Martha said ("You must have fallen asleep") don't form a question; the sentence as a whole does. The question mark goes *outside* the closing quotation marks to show the reader that. Look at this example:

▶ Martha actually said, "You must be right"!

Again, the actual words that Martha said don't form an exclamation; the sentence as a whole does, so the exclamation mark goes *outside* the closing quotation marks.

What do you do when both the sentence as a whole *and* the

words being quoted form a question or an exclamation? Use only *one* end mark (question mark or exclamation mark) and put it *inside* the closing quotation marks. Look at this example:

▶ Did I hear Martha say, "Who called this afternoon?"

Single Quotation Marks

In the United States, **single quotation marks** are used for a quotation within a quotation:

▶ "Mark said, 'I'll be fine,' but then he collapsed," cried Shameka.

▶ "I'm reading the story 'Plaid Blazers and Other Mysteries,'" said Laura.

What Mark said ("I'll be fine") and the name of the short story ("Plaid Blazers and Other Mysteries") would normally be enclosed with double quotation marks. But since these phrases come inside material that already is in double marks, you let the reader know where the quotation (or title) begins by using a single quotation mark.

Using Apostrophes

People often become confused about the purpose of apostrophes and end up using them in all sorts of creative ways. You can walk into almost any store and see signs like the following with incorrect uses of the apostrophe:

▶ Special price's this week!   Rent two movie's today!   Five can's for $4.00!

None of these words needs an apostrophe. Each is a simple plural, and you almost never need to use an apostrophe to denote a plural. Using an apostrophe need not be so difficult. Let's start with the easiest use of the apostrophe, the contraction.

Contractions

An apostrophe often indicates that at least one letter has been omitted from a word. This is called a contraction. For example, the contraction *don't* stands for *do not*; the *o* in *not* has been omitted. *I'll* is a form of *I will*; in this case the *wi* of *will* has been omitted.

Other examples:

Full Form	Contraction
is not	isn't
cannot	can't
she will	she'll
you have	you've
he is	he's

Possession

Before using an apostrophe, make sure that a phrase actually denotes possession and is not simply a plural. For instance, in the phrase *the babies' rattles*, the babies possess rattles (so an apostrophe is used); however, in the phrase *the babies in their cribs*, the babies are not possessing anything so an apostrophe is not needed.

Here are some guidelines to help you make sense of it all.

Guideline #1. If a singular noun doesn't end in *–s*, its possessive ends in *–'s*. Say what? Take a look at this sentence:

▶ The cars engine was still running.

The word *cars* needs an apostrophe to indicate possession, but where?

Use this mental trick to show where to place an apostrophe: Take the word that needs the apostrophe (*cars*) and the word that it's talking about (*engine*) and mentally turn the two words around so that the word you're wondering about is the object of a preposition such as *of*.

When you change *cars engine* around, you come up with *engine of the car.* Now look at the word *car.* *Car* is singular and doesn't end in *–s,* so the original should be punctuated *–'s.* You should have:

▶ The car's engine was still running.

Other examples of singular nouns with apostrophes:

▶ Shannon's book

▶ the lion's mane

▶ a book's pages

Guideline #2. When you have plural nouns that end in *–s* (and most do), add an apostrophe after the final *–s.* The same mental trick of turning the two words into a phrase applies.

Look at this sentence, which talks about two girls who have left behind their jackets:

▶ The girls jackets were left in the coatroom.

Now just apply the trick. Take the phrase *girls jackets,* and turn it around so that you have *jackets of (belonging to) the girls.*

When you've turned the phrase around this time, the word *girls* ends in *–s.* This lets you know that you should add an apostrophe after the *–s* in *girls,* so the sentence should read this way:

▶ The girls' jackets were left in the coatroom.

Other examples of plural nouns with apostrophes:

▶ five musicians' instruments

▶ twenty-four years' worth

▶ ten trees' branches

Although most English plurals end in *–s* or *–es,* there are a number of exceptions, such as *children, women,* and *deer.* If a plural doesn't end in *–s,* the possessive is formed with an *–'s* (that is, treat it as if it were singular).

▶ the children's coats

▶ the men's scores

▶ the oxen's yokes

One tricky part left to consider concerns singular words that end in –*s*. There are two ways of punctuating these words. Guideline #3 is used more often than Guideline #4, but you may want to ask your instructor or employer if there is a preference as to which you should follow.

Guideline #3. If a singular word ends in –*s*, form its possessive by adding –*'s* (except in situations in which pronunciation would be difficult, such as *Moses* or *Achilles*). Look at this sentence:

▶ Julie Jones help was invaluable in finding a new apartment.

Guideline #3 would tell you that, since *Jones* is singular and ends in –*s*, you'd show its possessive by adding –*'s*. Therefore, the sentence would be punctuated this way:

▶ Julie Jones's help was invaluable in finding a new apartment.

However, you may be told to use another rule:

Guideline #4. If a singular word ends in –*s*, form its possessive by adding an apostrophe after the –*s*. In this case, the sentence would be written this way:

▶ Julie Jones' help was invaluable in finding a new apartment.

Joint versus Individual Possession

There is a way to use apostrophes to show the reader whether the people you're talking about possess something jointly or individually. Take a look at this sentence:

▶ Jim and Allisons cars were stolen.

The question is, did Jim and Allison own the cars together or separately? If, say, Jim and Allison were a married couple and they had the misfortune of having two of their cars stolen, then the sentence would be punctuated in the following way:

▶ Jim and Allison's cars were stolen.

The possessive is used after the last person's name *only*. This usage tells the reader that Jim and Allison had joint ownership of the cars.

But say Jim and Allison were neighbors, and there was a rash of car thefts on their block. The sentence would then be punctuated this way:

▶ Jim's and Allison's cars were stolen.

The possessive is used after *both* names. This usage tells the reader that Jim and Allison had separate ownership of the cars.

Using an Apostrophe to Form a Plural: A Rare Occasion

Remember the store signs mentioned at the beginning of this section that incorrectly use an apostrophe:

▶ Special price's this week! Rent two movie's today! Five can's for $4.00!

The words that have apostrophes are just plain ol' plurals; they don't show ownership in any way and so don't need apostrophes. (If you're unsure about whether you should use an apostrophe, ask yourself if the word in question owns or possesses anything.)

There are a few rare instances when you use apostrophes to form plurals. The first is when you're writing abbreviations that have more than one period.

▶ M.D. = M.D.'s

Also, if you have proverbial expressions that involve individual letters or combinations of letters, use apostrophes to show their plurals.

▶ Dot your i's and cross your t's.

(In these instances, some style guides dictate that you shouldn't italicize the letter you're making plural; other guides take the opposite view.)

Another time that you should use an apostrophe to form a plural is when your reader would be confused by reading an –s alone (for instance, when an –s is added to an individual letter or letter combination, to hyphenated compounds, or to numbers used as nouns).

▶ s = s's (instead of ss)

Commas

When readers see a **comma**, they know that there is a slight pause, and they can tell how particular words or phrases relate to other parts of the sentence. Take a look at this sentence:

▶ Will you call Mary Alice Lee and Jason or should I?

What's being said here? This sentence has entirely different meanings, depending on how commas are placed in it.

▶ Will you call Mary, Alice, Lee, and Jason, or should I?
▶ Will you call Mary Alice, Lee, and Jason, or should I?
▶ Will you call Mary, Alice Lee, and Jason, or should I?

Commas with a Series

If you have a series of items, use a comma to separate the items. For example:

▶ The new convertible 2001 Ford and Chevy pickup were involved in a wreck.

How many vehicles were involved? With the following punctuation, you'd see that three vehicles were involved.

▶ The new convertible, 2001 Ford, and Chevy pickup . . .

However, this punctuation shows that only two vehicles were involved

▶ The new convertible 2001 Ford and Chevy pickup . . .

Use a comma between two or more adjectives that modify a noun:

▶ The man in the torn, tattered jacket moved quickly through the crowded, unlit street.

If the first adjective modifies the idea expressed by the combination of subsequent adjectives and the noun, then you don't need commas. Look at this sentence:

▶ Many countries do not have stable central governments.

Since *central governments* would be considered a single unit, it is not necessary to separate it from the adjective modifying it *(stable)* with a comma.

If you're using *and, or,* or *nor* to connect the items in the series, don't use commas:

- ▶ The flag is red and white and blue.
- ▶ The flag might be red or white or blue.
- ▶ The flag is neither red nor white nor blue.

Commas with Compound Sentences

If you have two independent clauses (that is, two complete thoughts that could stand alone as sentences) and they're joined by *but, or, yet, so, for, and,* or *not* (remember the mnemonic *boysfan*), join them with a comma:

- ▶ It was more than three hours past lunchtime, and everybody was grumbling about being hungry.

The exception: You may eliminate the comma if the two independent clauses are short and if there would be no danger of confusion with the comma not in the sentence. For example:

- ▶ We filled up with gas and we went on our way.

If you have a simple sentence with a compound verb, don't put a comma between the verbs:

- ▶ I wanted to get some rest [no comma] but needed to get more work done.

Commas with Quoted Material

If a quoted sentence is interrupted by words such as *he said* or *she replied*, use commas in this way:

- ▶ "For this contest," he said, "you need three pencils and two pieces of paper."

Note that the first comma goes before the closing quotation mark and the second comma goes before the beginning quotation mark.

If the words being quoted make up a question or an exclamation, don't include a comma:

> ▶ "Put that down right now!" Barry cried.

Commas with Clauses, Phrases, Appositives, and Introductory Words

Use commas to set apart clauses (groups of words that have a subject and a predicate), participle phrases, and appositives (words or phrases that give information about a noun or pronoun) that aren't necessary to the meaning of the sentence.

Take a look at this sentence:

> ▶ The handsome man over there, the only one who works in the deli department of the local supermarket, has black hair and brown eyes.

If you took out the clause *the only one who works in the deli department of the local supermarket*, you'd still have the same essential parts of the sentence. You don't need to know where the man works in order to learn his hair and eye color. Here's another way of looking at it: If you can take out the part you're questioning for commas and the sentence still makes sense, then you should use the commas. Now look:

> ▶ The only man who works in the deli department of the local supermarket was arrested for stealing four grapes and five apples.

In this case, if you removed *who works in the deli department of the local supermarket*, you'd have *The only man was arrested for stealing four grapes and five apples*. That isn't the meaning of the original sentence. *Remember:* If you need the extra words for the meaning, you don't need the commas.

Commas are also used after introductory words such as exclamations, common expressions, and names used in direct address that aren't necessary for the meaning of a sentence. If you have words that begin a sentence and you could understand the sentence without them, use a comma to separate them from the rest of the sentence.

For example:

▶ Why, don't you look nice tonight!

▶ Kayla, please help your brother find his tricycle.

▶ If you must know, I have been dyeing my hair for the past ten years.

A comma is also used before these same types of words and phrases when they appear at the end of a sentence, as long as they're not necessary for the meaning:

▶ Don't you think that new CD really rocks, Jean-Marie?

▶ You'll be coming with us to the company picnic on Sunday, I hope.

Use commas around words that interrupt a sentence (these are called **parenthetical expressions**), as long as the words aren't necessary for the meaning:

▶ The answer to the next question, Paula, can be found on page thirty-six.

▶ This textbook, unlike the one I had before, is written in a style I can understand.

Use a comma after an introductory verbal (remember that a verbal is a participle, gerund, or infinitive) or verbal phrase:

▶ Weeping at the sight of the destruction, the news reporter broke down on camera.

▶ To try to regain his composure, he took several deep breaths.

Use a comma after an introductory adverb clause. (Remember that an adverb clause is a group of words that has a subject and a verb, and that describes a verb, adjective, or other adverb.) For example:

▶ Because I didn't stop at the red light, I got a ticket.

▶ If Glenn comes in town tonight, the whole family is going to get together for a picnic.

Commas in Addresses

When writing out a mailing address as text (not on separate lines), put a comma between the person's last name and the start of the street address, then after the street address, then between the city and the state. It is not customary to put a comma between the state and the zip code. For example:

▶ Please remit the payment to Abby Householder, 4238 Old Highway 41 North, Hebbardsville, KY 42309.

If you're putting address information on separate lines, use a comma only between the city and state:

▶ Abby Householder
  4238 Old Highway 41 North
  Hebbardsville, KY 42309

If you mention a city and state in text, or a city and country, put commas around the state or country:

▶ I have to visit Clinton, Iowa, on my next sales trip.
▶ She is going to school in Grenoble, France, next spring.

Other Uses for Commas

1. Put a comma after the day of the week (if you've stated it), the day of the month, and the year (if the sentence continues):

▶ I'll be seeing you on Friday, February 23, 2001, at half past seven.

If you're writing only the day and month or the month and year, no comma is necessary:

▶ I'll see you on February 23.
▶ I'll see you in February 2002.

2. Put a comma after the greeting (salutation) of all friendly letters and the closing of all letters:

▶ Dear Aunt Aggie,
▶ Sincerely,

3. If a person's title or degree follows his or her name, put commas around it:

▶ Please call Robert Householder, Ph.D., at your convenience.

▶ The deposition was given by Edward Butterworth, M.D.

4. Using commas to divide numbers of 1,000 or more to make them easier to read:

▶ Is it my imagination, or are there 1,376,993 rules for commas?

Colons

A **colon** is used to introduce particular information. One of the most common uses of a colon is to signal to the reader that a list will follow:

▶ On the camping trip, please bring the following items: a flashlight, a sleeping bag, two boxes of matches, three changes of clothing, and food for six meals.

A colon is also used to explain or give more information about what has come before it in the sentence:

▶ There are a number of complaints that I have against the tenant: she tore the plaster in the living room, her dog stained the carpet in every room, and she has not paid her rent in three months.

In formal papers, a colon usually precedes a lengthy quotation:

▶ In his Gettysburg Address, Abraham Lincoln stated:

Four score and seven years ago, our forefathers brought forth upon this continent a new nation, conceived in liberty, and dedicated to the proposition that all men are created equal.

There are other times when a colon is used:

- In the greeting of a business letter
  - ▶ To Whom It May Concern:
- Between the hour and minutes in time
  - ▶ a meeting at 4:15 P.M.
- In dividing a title from its subtitle
  - ▶ *My Favorite Punctuation Marks: Why I Love Colons*
- In naming a chapter and verse of the Bible
  - ▶ Genesis 2:10
- In naming the volume and number of a magazine
  - ▶ *Time* 41: 14
- In naming the volume and page number of a magazine
  - ▶ *U.S. News and World Report* 166: 31
- Between the city and the publisher in a bibliographical entry
  - ▶ London: Covent Garden Press

Semicolons

A **semicolon** signals a pause greater than one indicated by a comma but less than one indicated by a period. The most common use for a semicolon is joining two complete thoughts (independent clauses) into one sentence.

Look at the following sentences:

▶ The bank teller determined the bill was counterfeit. There was no serial number on it.

Each of these sentences stands alone, but they could be joined by using a semicolon:

▶ The bank teller determined the bill was counterfeit; there was no serial number on it.

Often semicolons are used with conjunctive adverbs and other transitional words or phrases, such as *on the other hand* or *therefore*. In this case, be sure that you put the semicolon at the point where the two thoughts are separated. For example:

▶ **Right:** Traffic is worse than we expected; therefore, we won't be home before midnight.

▶ **Wrong:** Traffic is worse than we expected, therefore; we won't be home before midnight.

Now, it's time to break a rule about semicolons. There are times when a semicolon is used when a comma would seem to be the correct punctuation mark. Look at this sentence:

▶ The manhunt took place in Los Angeles, Nashville, Indiana, Stratford, Connecticut, Winnenan, Oklahoma, Dallas, and Olympia.

Notice that there are commas after the name of each city and each state. However, the reader will probably be confused about the true meaning of the sentence. Consider that a semicolon is a "notch above" a comma. By substituting a semicolon in places where you'd ordinarily use a comma, you make things clearer by showing which cities go with which states. Look at how the sentence should be punctuated:

▶ The manhunt took place in Los Angeles; Nashville, Indiana; Stratford, Connecticut; Winnenan, Oklahoma; Dallas; and Olympia.

Reading the sentence this way, the reader can tell that the manhunt took place in Nashville, Indiana, as opposed to Nashville, Tennessee. Also, the reader can identify that Winnenan is located in Oklahoma.

When Semicolons Won't Work

Semicolons won't work if the two thoughts are not on the same playing field (that is, if they're not logically connected). Look at these two sentences:

▶ The teller wore a blue suit. The police were called immediately.

Although both are sentences, there's no link between them. If a semicolon were used between these two sentences, readers would be scratching their heads, thinking they were missing something.

Semicolons also won't work if one of the thoughts is not a complete sentence. Look at this example:

▶ The police were called immediately; screeching through the streets.

The first part of the sentence is a complete thought *(the police were called immediately)*, but the second part is not *(screeching through the streets)*.

Hyphens

A **hyphen** is a short horizontal line (next to a zero on a keyboard); a dash is longer. But the differences between these two punctuation marks go much deeper than just a few fractions of an inch.

The most common use of the hyphen is to divide words at the ends of lines. The important rule to remember is to divide words only between syllables.

If you're not sure of where the syllables occur, consult a dictionary. In addition, most word processing software contains automatic hyphenation tools that you may use. One-syllable words should not be divided.

No matter where the words are divided, be careful to leave more than one letter at the end of a line (and more than two at the beginning of a line). You should also avoid hyphenating acronyms (such as UNESCO or NAACP), numerals (such as 1,200 or 692), and contractions (such as *haven't, didn't, couldn't*). Keep in mind that some style guides may say that proper nouns (those that are capitalized) should not be hyphenated.

Also try to avoid dividing an Internet or e-mail address. These addresses often contain hyphens as part of the address, so an extra hyphen would confuse the reader. If angle brackets (described later in this chapter) are not used, extending the address to the second line without any extra punctuation would make the address clear for your reader. You should do that this way:

▶ When I tried to order, I was directed to this site: *www.anglosaxon.com/rebates/year/1066/*.

Hyphens with Numbers

Use a hyphen (not a dash) between two dates and between page numbers:

▶ Prohibition (1919–1933) came about as a result of the Eighteenth Amendment.

▶ See the section on the Roaring Twenties (pp. 31–35) for more information.

Technically, both of these instances use what's called an "en dash," which is longer than a hyphen and shorter than a normal dash, which is usually called an "em dash." Most word processing programs have an "Insert" icon or a character map that you can use to access en and em dashes, as well as other symbols.

Another common use of the hyphen comes when numbers are written as words instead of numerals. The rule is to hyphenate numbers from twenty-one to ninety-nine.

Hyphens with Compound Adjectives

When a compound adjective (two or more adjectives that go together to form one thought or image) precedes the noun it modifies, it should be hyphenated. Look at these sentences:

▶ Charles Dickens was a nineteenth-century writer.

In this case, *nineteenth-century* is used as an adjective (it modifies the noun *writer*), and so it's hyphenated. Notice the difference:

▶ Charles Dickens was a writer who lived in the nineteenth century.

Here, *nineteenth century* is a noun, and so it's not hyphenated.

▶ Some well-known scientists are studying the effects of global warming.

In this example, *well-known* is used as an adjective before the noun *scientists,* and so it is hyphenated.

▶ Some scientists studying the effects of global warming are well known.

Since *well known* follows the noun here, it is not hyphenated.

Another situation in which you don't hyphenate a compound modifier—even if it comes before the noun—is where the first modifier is the word *very* or an adverb that ends in *–ly*. You should write:

▶ a very condescending attitude
▶ a strictly guarded secret
▶ a very little amount of money
▶ the highly publicized meeting

Use a hyphen to join adjectives only if together they form the same image. If they're separate words describing a noun (as *big, bulky package*), then don't use a hyphen. Take a look at this example:

▶ The candidate succeeded because of his many influential, fat-cat supporters.

Fat and *cat* go together to form the image that describes the supporters, so they're hyphenated. If the hyphen were not there, then the reader would see *fat cat supporters* and might wonder if the candidate really relied on *fat supporters* and *cat supporters.*

Hyphens for Clarification

Sometimes hyphens are needed to clarify the meaning of a sentence. For instance:

▶ Your favorite sports star resigned!

Should you be elated or upset? The way the sentence is punctuated now the star will no longer play. If, however, what the writer intended to get across was that the star had signed another contract, the sentence should contain a hyphen and be written this way:

▶ Your favorite sports star re-signed!

Other words with this idiosyncrasy include *recreation* and *recollect*.

Dashes

A **dash** provides a window for some informality in writing, allowing the writer to introduce a sudden change in thought or tone. Look at this sentence:

▶ The odometer has just reached thirty thousand miles, and I suppose it's time to call the garage to schedule a—oops! I just passed the street where we were supposed to turn.

The dash tells the reader that a sudden idea has interrupted the speaker's original thought.

A dash may also be used to give emphasis to something that's come before:

▶ Elizabeth spent many hours carefully planning what she would pack in the van—the van that would be her home for the next three months.

Another time a dash may be used is in defining or giving more information about something in the sentence. Read this sentence:

▶ Margaret knew that when she finally arrived at her sorority house, she would be warmly greeted by her sisters—Lillian, Bea, Kwila, and Arlene.

The last example could also be punctuated by using parentheses or a colon in place of the dash, as in these sentences:

▶ Margaret knew that when she finally arrived at her sorority house, she would be warmly greeted by her sisters (Lillian, Bea, Kwila, and Arlene).

▶ Margaret knew that when she finally arrived at her sorority house, she would be warmly greeted by her sisters: Lillian, Bea, Kwila, and Arlene.

Punctuating the sentence with colons is stuffier than using a dash or parentheses. Generally speaking, save the colon for formal writing.

Parentheses

Using **parentheses** tells the reader that you're giving some extra information, something that isn't necessary to the meaning of the sentence but is helpful in understanding what's being read. For example:

▶ For a complete study of Hitchcock's movies, consult Chapter 8 (pages 85–96).

Keep in mind that if the information is necessary for the sentence to be read correctly, you shouldn't use parentheses. For instance, if you're comparing statistics about two floods that occurred in different years, you might have a sentence like this:

▶ The high-water mark of the 1999 flood came in early April, as compared to the high-water mark of the 1956 flood, which occurred in late May.

You can't put *of the 1999 flood* or *of the 1956 flood* in parentheses because you need that information for the sentence. However, if you have a sentence written like this:

▶ My latest (and, I hope, my last) adventure with blind dates was a month ago; I haven't recovered yet.

You could omit the material inside the parentheses and you'd still have the essence of the sentence.

Another time parentheses are commonly used is in giving dates, especially birth and death dates.

▶ Dame Agatha Christie (1890–1976) wrote twelve novels that featured Miss Marple.

In addition, parentheses are used to enclose numbers or letters that name items in a series. Sometimes both the parentheses marks are used, and sometimes just the mark on the right-hand side is used:

▶ Before checking the patient, you should (a) wash your hands; (b) make sure the patient's chart is nearby; (c) call for the attending nurse to supervise.

or

▶ Before checking the patient, you should a) wash your hands; b) make sure the patient's chart is nearby; c) call for the attending nurse to supervise.

Whether you use both parentheses or just one, be consistent when you're naming items in a series. Also, be aware that if you use one parenthesis only, it's easy to get the letter mixed up with the preced-ing word.

Parentheses are also used to give a legislator's party affiliation and home state (in the case of national politics) or city or county (in the case of state politics).

▶ Senator Abby Brackman (D-R.I.) met in her Washington office with a number of constituents, including Representative Mark Digery (R-Providence).

Another—though less common—use for parentheses is to show the reader that an alternate ending for a word may be read. Take a look at this sentence:

▶ Please bring your child(ren) to the company picnic.

Keep in mind that parentheses would not be used this way in more formal writing; the sentence would be reworded to include both *child* and *children*.

Square Brackets

One place where you'll see **square brackets** is in dictionaries, where they are used to show the history of the word being defined.

Another use is in making certain that quoted material is clear or understandable for the reader. Suppose you're quoting a sentence that contains a pronoun without its antecedent, as in this example:

▶ "He burst onto the party scene and began to take society by storm."

Just who is *he?* Unless the previous sentences had identified him, your readers wouldn't know. In that case, you'd use square brackets this way:

▶ "He [Justin Lake] burst onto the scene and began to take society by storm."

Along the same lines, you use brackets to alter the capitalization of something you're quoting so that it fits in your sentence or paragraph. For example:

▶ "[T]he river's bank has eroded sufficiently to warrant major repair."

Use brackets for quoted material only if their use doesn't change the meaning of what's being quoted.

If you need to give information that you'd normally put in parentheses—but that information is already in parentheses—use brackets instead. For example:

▶ The man who was responsible for the arrest (James Bradson [1885–1940]) was never given credit.

Normally, you put a person's birth and death dates in parentheses, but since those dates would be placed in material that's already in parentheses, you use brackets instead.

Depending on the type of writing that you do, you might need to add the Latin word *sic* to the information that you're quoting. *Sic* translates as "thus," or "so," or "in this manner"; it is used to show that what you're quoting has a mistake that you are copying. Look at the following sentence:

▶ "This painting was donated to the museum on September 31 [*sic*]."

Now, you know and I know that "thirty days hath September"—not thirty-one, as above. By using [*sic*] the reader can tell that you copied the mistake as it was written in the original form.

Most style guides allow you to use either brackets or parentheses to let the reader know that you've added italics to quoted material. The only rule is that you keep using the same device throughout the manuscript. Take your pick:

▶ The time of the accident is as *equally important* as is the date [italics added].

▶ The time of the accident is as *equally important* as is the date (italics added).

Italics and Underlining

What's the difference in meaning between underlining and italics? There isn't any. With the use of computers, clicking a button and italicizing a word is now just as easy as underlining it. But sometimes (when you're writing longhand or when you're using a typewriter), the option to italicize is not available. Just remember to use either underlining or italicizing consistently throughout your document.

The most common use of italicizing or underlining is in titles, but only titles of long works, such as books. For titles of short works—such as short stories, short poems, and essays—quotation marks are used. For example:

▶ *The Complete Sherlock Holmes* or <u>The Complete Sherlock Holmes</u>
   (title of a book)
▶ "The Adventure of the Speckled Band"
   (title of a short story)

Note that the titles of sacred books don't require any punctuation nor do books of the Bible.

▶ I read the Bible for a half an hour today.

▶ A copy of the Koran was on his bedside table.

Here's a more complete list of works that should be italicized (underlined):

- Book-length poems (note that most poems are not book-length): *Leaves of Grass*
- Plays: *A Raisin in the Sun*
- Operas: *Carmen*
- Movies: *Casablanca*
- Pamphlets: *What You Should Do Before You See the Doctor*
- Television programs (the title of an episode from a program would have quotation marks since it's shorter): *The X-Files*
- Works of art: *Mona Lisa*
- Long musical works (a CD would be italicized; a song from the CD would have quotation marks around it): *Greatest Love Songs of the Nineties*
- Magazines and newspapers (an article title from the magazine or newspaper would have quotation marks around it): *Time*
- Ships, aircraft, spacecraft, trains: *Titanic*, U.S.S. *Cole* (don't italicize the U.S.S.); *Spirit of St. Louis*; *Endeavor*

Keep in mind that articles (*a, an,* and *the*) are italicized (underlined) only when they're part of the actual title. For instance:

▶ I read Sharyn McCrumb's book *The Rosewood Casket*.

The is part of the title of the book. On the other hand, you would write:

▶ I spent time aboard the *Mir* spacecraft.

Mir is the name of the spacecraft; *the* is not part of its name.

Be careful to apply italics (underlining) only to punctuation (commas, periods, question marks, exclamation marks, and the like) if that punctuation is part of the title.

▶ May screamed, "There's never been a better mystery than *The Murder of Roger Ackroyd*!"

The exclamation point and the ending quotation mark aren't italicized, since they aren't part of the title of the book.

Adding Emphasis

Look at the following sentences and see if you can tell the difference:

▶ "I'm *certain* I'm going to have to arrest you," he said slyly.

▶ "I'm certain *I'm* going to have to arrest you," he said slyly.

▶ "I'm certain I'm going to *have* to arrest you," he said slyly.

▶ "I'm certain I'm going to have to arrest *you*," he said slyly.

▶ "I'm certain I'm going to have to arrest you," he said *slyly*.

Can you see that the only difference in the five sentences is the words that are italicized? The use of italics tells the reader where emphasis should be placed. This helps the writer let the reader know the speech patterns being used, and it also helps the reader understand those patterns.

Be careful not to overuse italics (underlining) for emphasis, or you'll lose the emphasis you want to communicate. Look at this sentence:

▶ "Chief, the *culprit* is *Mark*, not *me*. I wasn't *there* when the *wreck* happened," Bill cried *sullenly* to the policeman.

With so many words italicized, the emphasis has lost its effectiveness.

Indicating a Different Context

Read the following sentence and see if it makes sense to you:

▶ The angry newspaper editor said to the young reporter, "You imbecile! You used robbery when you should have used burglary."

Say what? Is the editor telling the reporter that he or she committed the wrong crime? No, and if the writer had used the correct punctuation marks, then the sentence would make sense.

The rule is that when words, numbers, or letters are used outside of their normal context, they should be italicized (underlined). So the sentence really should be written this way:

▶ The angry newspaper editor said to the reporter, "You imbecile! You used *robbery* when you should have used *burglary*."

Written this way, the reader understands that the reporter used the words *robbery* and *burglary* incorrectly in his or her story.

You'll also apply this rule if you're reproducing a sound through a word (if you're using a form of onomatopoeia), as in

▶ *Brrr!* I didn't know it was this cold outside.

or

▶ When Jerri dropped her new calculator on the floor, she cringed as it went *kerplunk* when it landed.

Foreign Terms

One last use of italics (or underlining) is related to the previous one. This rule says you should italicize (or underline) a foreign word or phrase.

▶ I was wavering about whether to go to the festival with my friends, but I decided *carpe diem*.

If a foreign word or phrase has become so widely used in English that there wouldn't be any question of its meaning (like per diem or summa cum laude), there's no need to italicize it.

Angle Brackets

Years ago, you'd see **angle brackets** used only in a mathematical context, with > being the symbol for "greater than" and < being the symbol for "less than." Today, angle brackets are often used before and after

URLs (Internet addresses). Everything within the angle brackets should be copied exactly as it is in order for the address to work.

Many URLs contain miscellaneous marks of punctuation, including hyphens and periods, so determining whether a particular punctuation mark is part of the URL is not easy. Look at this sentence:

▶ Be sure to check out the information about this book and lots of our other fine publications at <www.-i-love-angle-brackets.net/ ~angle.brackets>.

By putting the URL inside brackets this way, the reader can tell that the closing period is the end of the sentence and isn't part of the URL. As an another option, Internet addresses can also be italicized; be sure to choose only italics or angle brackets (not both) and be consistent throughout your text.

Ellipsis Points

When **ellipsis points** or **marks** (three spaced periods) are used, the reader knows that some material from a quotation has been omitted. Look at this sentence:

▶ "Mary Jean left the game early because she felt that the team had no way of winning and she had a terrible headache," said Kathy Ann.

If you needed to quote that sentence, but the part about the team having no chance of winning had no relevance to what you were saying, you could use ellipsis points in this way:

▶ "Mary Jean left the game early because . . . she had a terrible headache," said Kathy Ann.

Note that you should use ellipsis points only if the meaning of the sentence isn't changed by what you omit. If the material you are omitting occurs at the end of a sentence, or if you omit the last part of a quoted sentence but what is left remains grammatically complete, you would use four ellipsis points, with the first one functioning as a period. Take this original passage:

▶ "A number of new people have joined the secret club. In fact, its membership has never been higher. Because the club is devoted to reading classical literature, however, its secret enrollment numbers have not been questioned by the public at large."

You could use ellipsis marks in these ways:

▶ "A number of new people have joined the secret club. . . . Because the club is devoted to reading classical literature, however, its secret enrollment numbers have not been questioned by the public at large."

or

▶ "A number of new people have joined. . . . [M]embership has never been higher. Because the club is devoted to reading classical literature, however, its secret enrollment numbers have not been questioned by the public at large."

Another use for ellipsis marks is in quoting someone and trying to show that there's a deliberate pause in what the person said, as in the following paragraph:

▶ Jimmy thought to himself, "If I can just hold on to the ball long enough to get it over to Mike, I know he can get the shot off. . . . I have to pace myself and keep watching the clock. . . . Twenty-five seconds . . . Fifteen seconds . . . Eight seconds . . . Time for a pass."

The Slash/Virgule/Solidus

A **slash** (also called a *virgule* or a *solidus*) is commonly used to mean *or.* Thus:

▶ a slash/virgule/solidus = a slash or virgule or solidus
▶ You may bring your spouse/significant other to the picnic. = You may bring your spouse or significant other to the picnic.

Some other uses of the slash are the following.

1. In mathematics, the slash is used to mean *per*, as in this sentence:
   ▶ There are 5,280 feet/mile.

2. A slash is used to form fractions:
   ▶ 9/16 (meaning 9 divided by 16)

3. In literature, the slash separates lines of poetry that are written in a block style, as in this passage from Edgar Allan Poe's "The Raven":
   ▶ Once upon a midnight dreary, while I pondered, weak and weary, / Over many a quaint and curious volume of forgotten lore— / While I nodded, nearly napping, suddenly there came a tapping, / As of some one gently rapping, rapping at my chamber door—/ "'Tis some visitor," I muttered, "tapping at my chamber door—/ Only this and nothing more. . . ."

4. With the popularity of the Internet, a common use of a slash is in URLs.
   ▶ His home page is at <www.myownwebsite.com/MarkPhillips/home>.

Chapter 7

Writing Better Sentences

If a sentence contains a misplaced or dangling modifier or is essentially illogical, it becomes confusing at best and ludicrous at worst. Some brief sentences, called fragments, are not proper sentences at all. At the other extreme, a writer may sometimes string several thoughts together to create a seemingly endless run-on sentence.

This chapter will give you some pointers for looking critically at your sentence construction and the tools to fix any problems you find.

Misplaced Modifiers

Simply put, **misplaced modifiers** are words or phrases that you've put in the wrong place. All modifiers should be as close as possible to whatever they describe or give more information about. Take a look at the following sentence.

▶ After her wreck, Joanna could comprehend what the ambulance driver was barely saying.

The way the sentence is written, the ambulance driver is barely speaking—but surely that's not what the writer meant. *Barely* should be moved so that it modifies the verb *could comprehend*. The sentence should be written this way:

▶ After her wreck, Joanna could barely comprehend what the ambulance driver was saying.

Misplaced modifiers can also be phrases, as in this example:

▶ Witnesses reported that the woman was driving the getaway car with flowing black hair.

A car with flowing black hair? Really? *With flowing black hair* is in the wrong place and should be moved as follows:

▶ Witnesses reported that the woman with flowing black hair was driving the getaway car.

One of the most common problems with misplaced modifiers comes with what are called limiting modifiers—words like *almost, even, hardly, just, merely, nearly, only* (*only* is the one misplaced most often), *scarcely,* and *simply.* To convey the correct meaning, limiting modifiers must be placed in front of the words they modify. Take a look at this sentence:

▶ Richard has nearly wrecked every car he's had.

Has Richard *nearly wrecked* the cars—in which case, he should be grateful for his luck—or has he wrecked *nearly every car*? Watch out for misplaced modifiers (to avoid wrecking nearly every sentence you write).

Dangling Modifiers

Dangling modifiers have no word or phrase to describe; they just dangle, or hang, in the sentence without something to hold on to. Take a look at these sentences:

▶ Long ears drooping on the floor, Julie wondered how the dog could walk.

Is it time for Julie to consider plastic surgery?

▶ While performing, the audience gasped as the singer forgot the words to the song.

Why was the audience performing? The above sentences need to be reworded so that the modifiers have something to attach to.

▶ Julie wondered how the dog could walk with its long ears drooping on the floor.

▶ The audience gasped as the singer forgot the words to the song while he was performing.

Squinting Modifiers

Squinting modifiers (sometimes called two-way modifiers) are words that can logically modify something on either side of them, but the reader can't be sure what the words modify:

▶ The instructor said after the semester ended that Mark was eligible to retake the test.

What does *after the semester ended* apply to? Did the instructor *tell* Mark this after the semester ended, or was Mark *eligible* to retake the test after the semester ended? To correct this sentence, change the placement of the modifier.

▶ After the semester ended, the instructor said that Mark was eligible to retake the test.

or

▶ The instructor said that Mark was eligible to retake the test after the semester ended.

Parallelism in Writing

Using **parallelism** means that you write all the similar parts of a sentence in the same way. If you've used two nouns, don't suddenly switch to a gerund. If you've used verbs that have a certain tense, don't suddenly change tenses.

Here are some of the rules for writing with parallel constructions.

1. *When naming items, present them all in the same way.* Look at this problem sentence:

▶ This afternoon I washed *[past tense verb with –ed]*, waxed *[past tense verb with –ed]*, and then I was vacuuming *[past progressive tense verb with –ing]* the car.

Now, here is the repaired sentence that's now parallel:

▶ This afternoon I washed, waxed, and vacuumed the car.

2. *When using more than one clause, keep the same voice and type of introduction in each.* Here is the problem sentence:

▶ I was worried that Bill would drive too fast *[active voice]*, that the road would be too slippery *[active voice]*, and that the car would be stopped by the police *[passive voice]*.

To make the sentence parallel, the last clause can be changed to the active voice:

▶ I was worried that Bill would drive too fast, that the road would be too slippery, and that the police would stop the car.

3. *Place items in a series in similar locations.* Take a look at this sentence:

▶ Mike is not only very kind but also is very good-looking.

Let's look at the problem:

▶ Mike is not only *[correlative conjunction **not only** comes after the verb]* very kind but also *[correlative conjunction **but also** comes before the verb]* is very good-looking.

Here's the repaired sentence that's now parallel:

▶ Mike is not only very kind but also very good-looking.

4. *Order items in a series by chronology or degree of importance.*
Look at this problem sentence:

▶ Misuse of the drug can result in fever, death, or dizziness.

Now, identify the problem:

▶ Misuse of the drug can result in fever *[something that's bad]*, death *[something that's the worst of the three]*, or dizziness *[something that's bad]*.

Here's the repaired sentence that's now parallel:

▶ Misuse of the drug can result in fever, dizziness, or death.

5. *Use prepositions for items in a series consistently and correctly.*
Let's look at this problem sentence:

▶ I hope to see you on November 20, December 13, and on January 7.

Here, the preposition *on* occurs before the first and third items in the series. To be consistent, delete the *on* before *January 7*. The first *on* will then apply to all the items in the series.

If different prepositions apply to items in a series, be sure to include all the correct prepositions:

▶ The invading ants are on the living room floor, the dining room table, and the sink.

The preposition normally used before *the sink* would be *in,* not *on.* Here's the repaired sentence:

▶ The invading ants are on the living room floor, on the dining room table, and in the sink.

6. *Sentences constructed in a parallel way are often more effective.*
Look at this example:

▶ I was nervous and frightened, but I hid my emotions. My sister showed the world that she felt confident and carefree.

There's no grammatical mistake with the sentences, but they can certainly be improved by being written in a parallel manner, as below.

▶ I was nervous and frightened, but I hid my emotions. My sister was confident and carefree, but she showed the world how she felt.

Writing Logically

No matter how meticulous you are in crafting the grammar and punctuation of your sentences, if your material has errors in logic, all your hard work will have been for nothing. As you write, keep the following common mistakes in mind.

1. **Faulty predication** occurs when your subject and verb don't make sense together (that is, the subject can't "be" or "do" the verb). Take a look at this sentence:

▶ The new breath mint assures customers that it will last all day.

Obviously, a breath mint is incapable of assuring anybody of anything. This sentence needs to be reworded:

▶ The makers of the new breath mint assure customers that the mint will last all day.

2. **Faulty coordination** occurs if you join (combine or coordinate) two clauses in an illogical way:

▶ I made my way to the head of the checkout line, yet I realized I had forgotten my wallet.

The word *yet* is used incorrectly. The sentence should read:

▶ I made my way to the head of the checkout line, but then I realized I had forgotten my wallet.

Another example of faulty coordination comes in sentences that contain independent clauses of unequal importance:

▶ I paid $50,000 for my new car, and it has tinted glass.

The cost of the car is more important than the fact that it has tinted glass. To correct the problem, you could make the second clause subordinate to the first.

▶ I paid $50,000 for my new car, which has tinted glass.

3. **Absolute adjectives** are words that cannot be compared. *Round*, for instance—something is either round or it's not.

Other absolute adjectives include the following:

blank	eternal	square	unique
complete	favorite	straight	vacant
dead	permanent	true	
empty	pure	unanimous	

Look at this example:

▶ I hadn't studied for the test; the paper I turned in was somewhat blank.

You can't have a paper that is somewhat blank; either it has something on it or it doesn't. Since these are words that can't be compared, be sure not to use *more, most, quite, rather, somewhat, very,* and other qualifiers in front of them.

4. **Faulty comparison** occurs if you compare two unlike people, places, or things:

▶ The traffic mishaps in April were more numerous than May.

This sentence compares mishaps to May, which makes no sense. The sentence should be rewritten like this:

▶ The traffic mishaps in April were more numerous than the mishaps in May.

Another problem is an ambiguous comparison that could be interpreted two different ways. Look at this sentence:

▶ Dawn dislikes traveling alone more than Dave.

The reader isn't sure what the word *more* applies to. Does Dawn dislike traveling alone more than she dislikes Dave, or does she dislike it more than Dave does?

5. **Sweeping (or hasty) generalizations** use all-encompassing words like *anyone, everyone, always, never, everything, all, only,* and *none,* and superlatives like *best, greatest, most, least.*

▶ The country never recovers from an economic downturn in just one week.

Be careful with sentences with generalizations like this one. What happens to the writer's credibility if the country does, in fact, recover from a downturn in one week? One possible rewording of the example is this:

▶ The country almost never recovers from an economic downturn in one week.

6. A **non sequitur** states an effect that doesn't logically follow from its cause.

▶ I turned in a paper; therefore, I'll pass the class.

As any teacher can tell you, turning in a paper doesn't necessarily mean that you will pass the class. What if the paper is not on the assigned topic or is plagiarized? Here are other non sequiturs:

▶ I've bought products made by Commonwealth Foods for years. Their new product, Dog Biscuits for Humans, is bound to be tasty.

▶ Jack stole a box of paper clips from the office. He probably cheats on his taxes, too.

7. One frequent mistake in logic comes from **omitting necessary words in comparisons**. Read this sentence:

▶ Aunt Lucy likes Cousin Louise more than she likes anyone in the family.

The way the sentence is written, Cousin Louise isn't in the family. The sentence needs to be reworded this way:

▶ Aunt Lucy likes Cousin Louise more than she likes anyone else in the family.

Sometimes sentences need the word *than* or *as* in order for them to be logical:

▶ Steve said he could play the guitar as well, if not better than, Jack.

Taking out the phrase *if not better than* leaves the illogical statement *Steve said he could play the guitar as well Jack.* The sentence should be written with the extra *as* to complete the phrase:

▶ Steve said he could play the guitar as well as, if not better than, Jack.

8. Another mistake in logic is commonly called **post hoc, ergo propter hoc,** which translates as *after this, so because of this.* Here the assumption is that because one thing follows another, the first caused the second.

▶ Terry washed her car in the morning, and it began to rain in the afternoon.

The second event was not caused by the first (although, come to think of it, it does seem to rain every time you wash your car, doesn't it?).

9. Other errors of logic include:

• A **false dilemma** (sometimes called an either/or fallacy) states that only two alternatives exist, when there are actually more than two:

▶ Mrs. Robertson can get to her appointment in one of two ways: she can either drive her car or she can walk. *(Mrs. Robertson has other choices: she could call a cab, take the bus, or ask a friend for a ride.)*

• A **red herring** dodges the real issue by citing an irrelevant concern as evidence:

▶ The driver in front of me ran the red light and was speeding, so it's not right that I get a ticket for going 100 mph in a 50 mph zone. *(What the driver ahead did is not relevant to whether or not the speaker's ticket was justified.)*

- **Circular reasoning** goes around in a circle (naturally), with nothing substantial in the middle. Here's an example:

▶ The epidemic was dangerous because everyone in town felt unsafe and at risk. *(The second part of the sentence provides no clarification about why the epidemic was dangerous.)*

Sentence Fragments

A **sentence fragment** is defined as "a group of words that is not a sentence." Okay, so what constitutes a sentence? Again, a sentence is a group of words that (1) has a subject, (2) has a predicate (verb), and (3) expresses a complete thought.

If a string of words doesn't meet all three qualifications, then you have a fragment. Take a look at these two words:

▶ Spot ran.

You have a subject *(Spot)*, a verb *(ran)*, and the words express a complete thought. Since you have all the requirements (subject, verb, complete thought), you have a sentence.

Now, look at this group of words:

▶ Although she had a new job in a modern office building.

This example is a subordinate clause that's punctuated as if it were a sentence. You have a subject *(she)* and a verb *(had)*, but what you don't have is a complete thought. If someone said only those words to you, you'd be left hanging. (Although she had a new job—what? She took off for the Far East? She called in sick on her first day?)

A participial phrase often creates another common sentence fragment, as below:

▶ Scared stiff by the intense wind and storm.

Who was scared stiff? Obviously, something's missing.

Read the following paragraph and see if you can spot the fragments.

▶ The lone woman trudged up the muddy riverbank. Determined that she would make the best of a bad situation. Because of her family's recent run of bad luck. She knew that she had to contribute to the family's finances. That's why she had accepted a teaching position. In this town that was new to her.

Did you spot all the fragments? Take a look at:
▶ Determined that she would make the best of a bad situation.
▶ Because of her family's recent run of bad luck.
▶ In this town that was new to her.

If you said those words alone, would anybody know what you meant? No—those words don't form complete thoughts.

Now, how can you correct these fragments? Usually the fragment should be connected to the sentence immediately before or after it—whichever sentence the fragment refers to. (A word of caution: Just be sure that the newly created sentence makes sense.)

Here's one way you could correct the paragraph to eliminate the fragments:

▶ Determined that she would make the best of a bad situation, the lone woman trudged up the muddy riverbank. She knew that, because of her family's recent run of bad luck, she had to contribute to the family's finances. That's why she had accepted a teaching position in this town that was new to her.

Note that to add variety to the paragraph, one fragment has been added to the beginning of one other sentence, one to the end, and one (*because of her family's recent run of bad luck*) was inserted in the middle of a sentence.

You generally shouldn't use fragments in formal writing; however, using them occasionally is okay for a casual writing style. Acceptable uses of a fragment include the following.

- In a short story or novel (but not excessively)
- When you're quoting someone
- In a bulleted or numbered list (like this one)
- To make a quick point—but only when the construction isn't confusing to the reader

Run-On Sentences

Another mistaken construction is a **run-on sentence**, which has at least two complete thoughts (two independent clauses, that is) but lacks the necessary punctuation between the thoughts.

One type of run-on, called a **fused sentence**, occurs when two (or more) sentences are fused together without a punctuation mark to show the reader where the break occurs. Take a look at this sentence:

▶ For our annual picnic, Tom and Jill brought hamburgers we brought potato salad.

In the sentence, there are two separate thoughts: *For our annual picnic, Tom and Jill brought hamburgers* and *we brought potato salad*. To make clear where one thought ends and another begins, you can:

▶ **Create two separate sentences:** For our annual picnic, Tom and Jill brought hamburgers. We brought potato salad.

▶ **Insert a semicolon:** For our annual picnic, Tom and Jill brought hamburgers; we brought potato salad.

▶ **Insert a comma and one of seven conjunctions—*but, or, yet, so, for, and, nor*:** For our annual picnic, Tom and Jill brought hamburgers, and we brought potato salad.

Another type of run-on is a **comma splice** (sometimes known as a comma fault), a sentence that has two complete thoughts that are spliced together by just a comma. Take a look at this sentence:

▶ Jamal wanted to go to the ball game, his friend Jason wanted to see the new movie.

On either side of the comma, you have a complete thought. You can correct the sentence with any of the three choices mentioned above.

▶ **Using a period:** Jamal wanted to go to the ball game. His friend Jason wanted to see the new movie.

▶ **Using a semicolon:** Jamal wanted to go to the ball game; his friend Jason wanted to see the new movie.

▶ **Adding a conjunction:** Jamal wanted to go to the ball game, but his friend Jason wanted to see the new movie.

You might also add a semicolon and a connecting word or phrase:

▶ Jamal wanted to go to the ball game; however, his friend Jason wanted to see the new movie.

Transitional Words and Phrases

Good writers rely on the use of **transitional words and phrases** (you might be more familiar with the terms *connecting words* or *parenthetical expressions*). Transitional words and phrases show your readers the association between thoughts, sentences, or paragraphs, and they help make your writing smoother. Look at the following paragraph:

▶ The blind date was a disaster. It was a complete debacle. I was intrigued by what my "friend" Sarah had told me about Bill; she had said that he was charming and was open to meeting someone new. He had recently seen me at a party and had wanted to meet me. Sarah said Bill was just my type. She said that he was an avid reader; we would have lots to talk about. He liked playing tennis; that was a plus for me. I had an earlier vow never to go out on another blind date. I agreed to meet Bill.

There's nothing wrong with the grammar, punctuation, or spelling in that paragraph, but it is choppy and boring. Now read the same paragraph after transitional words and phrases (underlined) have been added:

▶ The blind date was <u>more than</u> a disaster. <u>In fact</u>, it was <u>clearly</u> a complete debacle. <u>At first</u>, I was <u>somewhat</u> intrigued by what my "friend" Sarah had told me about Bill; <u>namely</u>, she had said that he was <u>quite</u> charming and <u>also</u> was open to meeting someone new. <u>In fact</u>, he had recently seen me <u>in the distance</u> at a party and had wanted to meet me. <u>Besides</u>, Sarah said, Bill was just my type. She said that he was <u>quite</u> an avid reader <u>for one thing</u>; <u>therefore</u>, we would have lots to talk about. <u>In addition</u>, he liked playing tennis; that was <u>certainly</u> a plus for me. <u>So, in spite of</u> my earlier vow never to go out on another blind date, I <u>eventually</u> agreed to meet Bill <u>on Saturday</u>.

Much better, isn't it? By including the transitions, the movement from one idea to another is much smoother, and the language of the paragraph has some life in it.

Classifying the Connectors

Transitional words and phrases can be divided into categories according to their use. The following should give you lots of ideas for adding transitional elements to your writing:

- **addition/sequence:** *additionally, afterward, again, also, and, and then, another . . . , besides, equally important, eventually, finally, first . . . second . . . third, further, furthermore, in addition, in the first place, initially, last, later, likewise, meanwhile, moreover, next, other, overall, still, too, what's more*
- **concession:** *admittedly, although it is true that, certainly, conceding that, granted that, in fact, it may appear that, naturally, no doubt, of course, surely, undoubtedly, without a doubt*
- **contrast:** *after all, alternatively, although, and yet, at the same time, but, conversely, despite, even so, even though, for all that, however, in contrast, in spite of, instead, nevertheless, nonetheless, nor, notwithstanding, on the contrary, on the other hand, or, otherwise, regardless, still, though, yet*

- **examples, clarification, emphasis:** *after all, an instance of this, as an illustration, by all means, certainly, clearly, definitely, e.g., even, for example, for instance, for one thing, i.e., importantly, indeed, in fact, in other words, in particular, in short, more than that, namely, of course, of major concern, once again, specifically, somewhat, such as, that is, that is to say, the following example, this can be seen in, thus, to clarify, to demonstrate, to illustrate, to repeat, to rephrase, to put it another way, truly, undoubtedly, without a doubt*
- **place or direction:** *above, adjacent to, at that point, below, beyond, close by, closer to, elsewhere, far, farther on, here, in the back, in the distance, in the front, near, nearby, neighboring on, next to, on the other side, opposite to, overhead, there, to the left, to the right, to the side, under, underneath, wherever*
- **purpose/cause and effect:** *accordingly, as a consequence, as a result, because, consequently, due to, for that reason, for this purpose, hence, in order that, on account of, since, so, so that, then, therefore, thereupon, thus, to do this, to this end, with this in mind, with this objective*
- **qualification:** *almost, although, always, frequently, habitually, maybe, nearly, never, oftentimes, often, perhaps, probably, time and again*
- **result:** *accordingly, and so, as a result, as an outcome, consequently, hence, so, then, therefore, thereupon, thus*
- **similarity:** *again, also, and, as well as, besides, by the same token, for example, furthermore, in a like manner, in a similar way, in the same way, like, likewise, moreover, once more, similarly, so*
- **summary or conclusion:** *after all, all in all, as a result, as has been noted, as I have said, as we have seen, as mentioned earlier, as stated, clearly, finally, in any event, in brief, in conclusion, in other words, in particular, in short, in simpler terms, in summary, on the whole, that is, therefore, to conclude, to summarize*
- **time:** *after a bit, after a few days, after a while, afterward, again, also, and then, as long as, as soon as, at first, at last, at length, at that*

time, at the same time, before, during, earlier, eventually, finally, first, following, formerly, further, hence, initially, immediately, in a few days, in the first place, in the future, in the meantime, in the past, last, lately, later, meanwhile, next, now, on (a certain day), once, presently, previously, recently, second, shortly, simultaneously, since, so far, soon, still, subsequently, then, thereafter, this time, today, tomorrow, until, until now, when, whenever

Chapter 8

Avoiding Common Errors

In a recent informal survey, copyeditors and English teachers were asked about mistakes they frequently encounter in print or speech. This chapter includes a rundown of the most common grammatical and stylistic errors, along with tips for avoiding them in your writing.

First, we'll discuss how to rid your writing of clichés, redundancies, wordiness, and the dreaded double negative. Then we'll take a look at lists from teachers and copyeditors of the most common, annoying, and—fortunately—avoidable writing and style errors.

Steering Clear of Clichés

A **cliché** is a worn-out expression, one you've heard over and over. In general, you should avoid using clichés because they're unoriginal, stale, and monotonous. Some examples include the following.

▸ costs an arm and a leg

▸ every cloud has a silver lining

▸ put all your eggs in one basket

To reword any cliché that makes its way into your writing, try "translating" it in a literal way. Say, for instance, that you've written:

▸ It was plain as the nose on his face that Drew wouldn't stick his neck out for anybody else.

In that sentence, you're dealing with two clichés *(plain as the nose on his face* and *stick his neck out).* To make the sentence cliché-free, you could change it to:

▸ Plainly, Drew wouldn't take a risk for anybody else.

Eliminating Repetition

Redundant words or phrases waste the reader's time. Here are some examples of some common redundant phrases, along with explanations of why they're redundant.

Redundant Phrase	Explanation
advance planning	Planning must be done in advance.
ask the question	It's impossible to ask anything except a question.
assembled together	It's impossible to assemble apart. Delete *together.*
cash money	Is cash ever anything but money?
combined together	Things that are combined must be together. Delete *together.*
each and every	The words mean the same thing; delete one.
end result	Can you have a result that's not in the end?
fewer in number	As opposed to fewer in what else?
green in color	As opposed to green in what?
large in size	The word *large* denotes size; use *large* only.
mix together	It's impossible to mix apart, isn't it?

Redundant Phrase	Explanation
month of May	Everybody knows that May is a month.
rectangular in shape	If something is rectangular, that is its shape.
same identical	Something that's identical must be the same. Delete one word or the other.
sum total	If you have a sum, you have a total. Delete one word or the other.

Cutting Out Wordy Expressions

Wordiness is the first cousin of redundant writing. Take a look at the following list of common wordy expressions, then get to work putting your words on a diet. For more common wordy expressions and their suggested substitutes, see Appendix B.

Wordy Phrase	Suggested Substitute
a small number of	a few
due to the fact that	since, because
give consideration to	consider
in a timely manner	promptly, on time
reach a conclusion	conclude, end, finish
until such time as	until
with regard to	concerning, about

Double Negatives

Now for the **double negative**; that is, two negative words that are used to stress denial or opposition. Examples of these include:

▶ After he was laid off, Hal realized that he didn't need none of the luxuries he'd become accustomed to.

(*Didn't* and *none* are negatives.)

▶ That man was not doing nothing but just standing there!

(*Not* and *nothing* are negatives.)

The way to correct a double negative is generally to change one of the negative expressions. For example, in the first example above, change *none* to *any:*

▶ After he was laid off, Hal realized that he didn't need any of the luxuries he'd become accustomed to.

One exception to the rule of avoiding double negatives is when you intend a positive or lukewarm meaning. Read this sentence:

▶ I was not unhappy with my recent raise.

The connotation in the double negatives *(not* and *unhappy)* tells the reader that, while the writer wasn't unhappy, he or she wasn't exactly over the moon either.

It's also fine to use double negatives if you're using a phrase or clause for emphasis, as in this example:

▶ "I will not take a bribe, not today, not tomorrow, not any time in my life," the politician cried.

And the Survey Says . . .

In a survey asking for examples of blunders they've seen in written work, copyeditors tended to focus on errors of grammar, spelling, and usage, while teachers were inclined to concentrate on the specifics of writing. Following each "complaint" are suggestions for eliminating these mistakes from your work.

Common Complaints from Copyeditors

1. **Omitted words or words put in the wrong place after cutting and pasting the text.** Reread your material—especially after you've cut and pasted. Use the techniques in Chapter 9 to proofread more effectively.

2. **Use of passive construction when the active voice would be appropriate—and would read better, too.** Unless there's a

particular need for the passive voice, rewrite sentences to use the active voice.

3. **Improper use of apostrophes (especially plural versus possessive).** Ask yourself if each apostrophe you are using has a legitimate use in a contraction or in showing possession. Pay particular attention to apostrophes used with *yours*, *his*, *hers*, *theirs*, *ours*, *its* (only *it's* ever takes an apostrophe, and only when you mean *it is*).

4. **Comma complaints.** Common transgressions include:
   ▶ Misplaced or omitted commas
   ▶ Commas inserted between a month and year (September, 2001)
   ▶ Commas dropped after parenthetical phrases (such as, "George Bush, president of the United States said he . . . ")
   ▶ Commas misused with restrictive and nonrestrictive clauses (no commas before *which*; commas before *that* used unnecessarily)
   ▶ Commas inserted between the subject and the verb (e.g., "The speeding car, was seen going through a red light")

5. **Number disagreements—either subject-predicate or antecedent-pronoun.** Look for each verb and its subject (or each pronoun and its antecedent); make sure that *both* of them are singular or *both* of them are plural.

6. **Use of *this* as a subject ("*This* can lead to confusion.").** Identify what *this* refers to and reword to eliminate *this* as a subject.

7. **Mistakes in word choice.** These include:
   ▶ Using *which* for *that* and vice versa
   ▶ Confusing *they're*, *their*, and *there*
   ▶ Confusing *your* with *you're*
   ▶ Using *between you and I* instead of *between you and me*

Teachers' Pet Peeves

1. **Difficulty grasping the concept of a topic sentence.** All of the other sentences in a paragraph should support the topic sentence or give examples to elaborate on it. If a sentence doesn't, eighty-six it.

2. **No transition from paragraph to paragraph in language or thought.** As you reread your work, ask yourself where you move from one point to another or from one example to another, then make connections with appropriate transitional words or phrases.

3. **Sentence fragments.** Read each sentence separately and ask yourself if the words in that sentence make sense when you read them alone. If they don't, your "sentence" is a fragment.

4. **No sense of who the audience is.** Common problems arise in the tone used and in addressing someone who is not part of the audience (for instance, writing "When you take freshman English . . . " when the audience—in this case, the instructor—is not taking freshman English).

5. **Inappropriate colloquial usages.** Look through your writing for slang words or idiomatic phrases. Unless your work calls for a relaxed or conversational tone, change to more formal language.

6. **Use of "non-sentences" that have lots of fluff but little substance.** (For example, "Language is important to everyday life and society.") Look for generalizations, clichés, and platitudes in your work. Reword your sentences to be more specific, to give more details, or to be less hackneyed.

Chapter 9

Getting Down to Business: Writing and Revising

If you're like many writers, you may find that the hardest part of writing is just getting started. The first sections of this chapter will provide you with a variety of methods for organizing your thoughts and getting your pen (or your computer keys) moving.

You'll then move—finally!—to creating your first draft. (Note the word "first.") When that is done, take advantage of the many tips here for revising and polishing your great work. No matter what type of writing you're doing, you can use this chapter to develop your own process for producing prose as graceful and error-free as possible.

Helpful Preliminaries

At the "prewriting" stage of the game, you can use one (or more than one) of the techniques discussed below to help you think clearly and keep track of your ideas. You'll probably come up with a number of ideas that you'll eventually discard. That's fine; what matters is getting your thoughts on paper. After that, you can go back and decide which ones are the keepers.

One way to organize your thoughts before you even begin the prewriting stage is to keep a journal. Whenever ideas come to you, jot them down in your journal. When the time comes for writing your first draft, you'll already have a number of ideas.

1. **Freewriting** is one of the most effective methods of cultivating ideas. Begin by writing your topic at the top of the page. Write anything related to your topic—words, phrases, or complete sentences, whatever scraps of thought come to mind. Give yourself a time limit of about ten minutes. Don't:

- Be concerned with spelling or punctuation
- Go to the time or trouble of grouping your ideas
- Bother erasing anything
- Worry even if you digress from your topic
- Stop if you can't think of a specific word (just write ??? or XXX or some other shorthand)

If you get stumped, just keep your pen moving on the paper or your fingers moving on the keyboard; chances are you'll come up with a new idea. At the end of your time allotment, look over your work. Decide what best fits with the direction of your work, and cross out what doesn't. Then go back and underline the key parts of the most workable ideas.

You can repeat the process to expand on the ideas that you like. Since you're working in ten-minute sessions, the assignment may not seem as overwhelming as it first did.

2. **Questioning** is another method to help you develop ideas. Suppose you've been given a very general topic like "relate a terrible dining experience you once had." Begin by asking yourself

variations of the reporter's fundamental six *w* and *h* questions (who? what? when? where? why? how?)

▶ Who was involved?

(you and your date Pat)

▶ What started the "horrible" part of the evening?

(you both became sick while still sitting at the table)

▶ When did this happen?

(on a summer evening in 2001)

▶ Where did this happen?

(at Sally's Scrumptious Shrimp Shack, in Seattle)

▶ Why did this happen?

(you had eaten seafood that hadn't been cooked long enough)

▶ How did the evening end at the restaurant?

(the manager gave you a complimentary dinner and a gift certificate to return another time)

After asking yourself other who? what? when? where? why? how? questions, you'll have compiled lots of details to give your readers a more descriptive picture of what happened that night.

3. In the prewriting strategy called **clustering** (also known as "mapping"), you use circles and lines to connect your thoughts. Begin by drawing a circle in the middle of your paper and writing your topic inside it. Then start thinking of random words or phrases associated with your topic. As you think of something, write it in a separate circle and connect it to the main idea with a line. As you think of ideas that are offshoots of the new circles, draw other circles, write the new information in them, and then connect them.

Don't worry about being messy or inartistic, and don't be concerned if you can't think of anything associated with some of the circles. (If you get stumped, ask yourself one of the who? what? when? where? why? how? questions.)

4. An **outline** is a kind of blueprint that helps you organize your thoughts in a logical pattern. You can use outlining as a prewriting method as a way of organizing the ideas you generated in freewriting, questioning, clustering, or any other technique.

Here's an example of a formal outline:

Contrast and Compare Watching a Movie in a Theater and at Home

A number of differences and similarities exist between watching a movie in a theater and watching a movie at home.

I. Differences
    A. Home
        1. Greater freedom
            a. More comfort
                (1) Can watch wearing pajamas, if I choose
                (2) Have choice of seating at home
                    (a) Can sit in favorite easy chair
                    (b) Can lie on floor or couch
            b. More choice of times to watch
                (1) Can stop to talk if phone rings
                (2) Can stop for bathroom breaks
                (3) Can stop if I want to get food or drink
        2. Fewer restrictions about food or drink
            a. Less expensive at home
            b. Open choice of food or drink
    B. Movie theater
        1. Much larger screen at movies
        2. Better popcorn at movies
        3. Earlier date for availability to be seen
        4. Better sound system
        5. Larger seating capacity, if needed for large group of friends

6. Better "maid service" (someone else picks up the discarded candy wrappers, etc.)

II. Similarities

A. *(Follow the same format to fill in details about the similarities between watching a movie at a theater and at home)*

1.

a.

(1)
(2)

(a)
(b)

b.

2.

B.

Each main entry begins with a Roman numeral. Then come the indented capital-letter entries *(Home* and *Movie Theater)* under each Roman numeral, and both are written in a parallel way (in this case, as nouns). Then come indented entries written with Arabic numbers, each begun with a comparative adjective *(Greater, Fewer, Larger, Better, Earlier)*. The entries go on—lowercase letters, then numbers inside parentheses, then lowercase letters inside parentheses—and each subcategory has a parallel grammatical layout.

Your First Draft

After you have your ideas in some form, it's time to write your first draft. The object is not to have something that's ready to turn in to your teacher, your supervisor, or your editor, but just to get all of your ideas down on paper in complete sentences.

In this phase, some writers prefer to begin thinking about mechanics, usage, and spelling, and others prefer to worry about the fine-tuning later. Do whatever works for you. Right now your main concerns are your purpose, your audience, and the format or type of writing that's required.

Defining Your Purpose

Almost all writing tries to prove a point, answer a question, give instructions, provide reflection, or present entertainment. Types of writing include:

- *Narrative* (telling a story)
- *Expository* (explaining or giving information)
- *Descriptive* (providing a written picture of someone, some-place, or something)
- *Informative or explanatory* (giving data or some other type of information)
- *Expressive* (detailing your thoughts or emotions)
- *Persuasive or argumentative* (attempting to influence others to come around to your way of thinking)
- *Analytical* (examining material presented to you)

Remember that you can improve most nonfiction by using lots of specific examples or supporting details. Take a look at this sentence, written for an essay about an ideal vacation spot:

▶ England is a good place to visit.

That sentence doesn't exactly make you want to pack your bags, does it? However, with a few details added, it becomes a workable sentence:

▶ From the jam-packed boulevards of cosmopolitan London, to the barely wide enough cobblestone paths of ancient York, to the right-for-rambling lanes of Lake District villages, olde England crooks its finger and beckons me.

Not only is it important that you know your purpose, you must also communicate it to your reader—preferably in your first few sentences. For example, reading the revised sentence about visiting England, you'd expect that the rest of the work would be about what a fascinating place England is to visit.

This sentence would be called your **thesis sentence** or **thesis statement**. If your writing format requires a thesis statement, keep in mind that every sentence of your work has to be connected to it in some way. After you've finished, look at each separate sentence or idea and ask yourself if it is somehow related to your thesis statement. If it isn't, cross it out.

It might help to keep a large copy of your thesis statement on a piece of paper close to your desk. Even for writing that doesn't require a thesis statement, you might find that writing a one-sentence statement of your purpose helps you center your thoughts.

Anticipating Your Audience

As a writer, you need to be aware of the audience for whom you're writing. You should keep certain things in mind, like the tone, vocabulary level, and style that's appropriate.

If you're writing a letter of complaint, for instance, you might use a far more aggressive tone (and maybe even a different level of vocabulary) than if you're writing for yourself, your business, or your instructor. Also, depending on what you're writing, your style could be formal, informal, or very casual.

In considering your audience, think about these questions:

- Are there age considerations that would mean you should write on a particular level?
- Will your audience expect extra information in your work, like quotations, citations, tables, or graphs? (These might be

needed in an academic or business paper.)

- Are there geographic considerations or cultural differences that you need to explain?
- Are your readers of a specific gender, or do they have a particular political or religious preference?
- What's the occupation of your audience?
- What need does your audience have for what you're writing?
- What information does your audience already have?
- What might your audience not be aware of?

Keep in mind that you don't want to insult your audience either by using inappropriate humor or by being patronizing or pretentious, so adjust your tone and your vocabulary accordingly.

Adhering to a Particular Style

The next part of your work is deciding the style or format to use. If you have an assignment from school or work, the style may have been decided for you. For example, for school you might be assigned to write a three-page essay critiquing a recent tax proposal, or at your business you may need to write a summary of the main points of a meeting you attended.

If a particular style is required, be sure you adhere to it. If you're unsure how to write in a particular style or format, look at successful past material and model your work after it.

Also, check to see if you're required to use a title, page numbers, headings, citations and other references, and a table of contents. If these are required, find out if they must be written in certain positions or in a specific way.

Revising Your Writing

Now, it's time to fine-tune your work by revising it. However, revising is much more than just looking for misspelled words and an errant comma or two. It entails looking at the big picture (organization, purpose, vocabulary, tone, and so on) as well as the little brush strokes of punctuation, usage, and spelling.

Making these improvements takes time, and you can usually count on writing more than one revision—sometimes even four or five revisions. I hope you haven't passed out from the shock of that idea, but the truth is, if you want your writing to be the best it can be, you need to devote a lot of time to the editing process.

General Questions to Ask

When taking a look at your first draft (or your second or third), you should consider a number of questions in order to determine if your writing is as good as it could be.

1. Begin by looking at your subject and your purpose in writing. What were you supposed to do in this piece? For instance, if you were supposed to argue against capital punishment, did you maintain that argument throughout or did you slip into an "on the other hand" approach and start giving opposing arguments?

2. Is it your introduction clear enough? Is your conclusion effective? Does it stray from the topic or your thesis statement? One helpful trick is to read your introduction and your conclusion (skipping the parts in between), and ask yourself if both are saying the same thing. If not, you need to revise.

3. If your piece of writing required a thesis, did you state it clearly? Did each of your supporting points relate to your thesis?

4. Have you presented all of your information coherently? Have you given enough examples, facts, or details to support each of your

points? If you gave examples in your work, did you explain why each example is significant? Do your examples follow each other in a logical order? Would adding anything strengthen your work?

5. Is your tone and language suitable for your audience?

6. Have you adhered to the formatting or style that was mandated? Do you have the prescribed margin sizes? font style? point size? spacing requirements? page numbering?

7. If your paper is about a literary work, have you stated the author's first and last names and the title of the work? Have you used the proper citation or documentation methods?

Particular Points to Look For

Once you make sure that your piece of writing has a firm structure on a sound foundation, it's time to look at it more closely.

1. Have you varied the length and structure of your sentences?

2. Could your wording be more concise, vivid, or explanatory?

3. Have you used any first- or second-person pronouns *(I, we, you, us)*? Is using them in writing acceptable in your class or workplace? Have you maintained a consistent point of view?

4. Do any related thoughts or sentences require a transitional word or phrase between them?

5. Have you used the active voice whenever possible? Also, look for sentences that begin with words like *it, this,* or *there;* these sentences can often become more forceful when you reword them.

6. Are there any synonyms that replace any repeated or imprecise words? Don't hesitate to consult a dictionary or thesaurus.

7. Is there any inappropriate slang or jargon or clichés in your work?

8. Some instructors and companies dictate that certain words not be used. If that applies to you, have you checked (on a computer, use the *Find* function) for those particular words or phrases?

After you've checked your paper for all these points, you'll probably need to rewrite parts of it. When you've done that, reread the section on revision above and apply it to your rewritten version. (Remember that warning that more than one revision would be necessary?)

A Final Reading

Hurray! You're almost home free. You've checked your content, your organization, and your sentence structure, and now you're ready to do some serious proofreading to help you find those little nitpicky errors that can change a masterpiece into a laughter piece.

The hints that follow will help to slow down your eyes so that they don't go faster than your brain. In other words, you read what you actually wrote rather than what you think you wrote.

1. **Read your paper out loud.** Out loud, you must read more slowly, so you'll often catch grammatical and spelling mistakes and similar constructions that you'd miss in silent reading.

2. **Read backward.** Start at the end and read the last sentence, then the sentence before that, and so on until you reach the beginning. When you read out of order, you'll more easily spot errors.

3. **Look for your most frequent past errors.** For instance, if you have trouble with sentence fragments, go back through your work and closely examine each sentence.

4. **Check your spelling yourself.** A spell checker will detect only words that are not in the dictionary. A good idea is to make one pass through your copy looking for spelling errors alone.

5. **Check your tense usage.** If you began your piece using the past tense, for example, make sure that you wrote the rest in the past tense (not including any quoted material, of course).

6. **Let someone else proofread and respond to your paper.** This is known as *peer editing*. Ask the other readers to be as critical as possible and to look for any kind of error—in spelling, punctuation, usage, mechanics, organization, clarity, even in the value of your ideas. Chances are if he or she had trouble reading or understanding your material, you should do some extra revision.

Chapter 10
Writing Formats: Essays, Summaries, Reports, and More

I f you're confused about a style of writing that you need to do—whether for a class, work, or just yourself—take a look at the various types of writing in this chapter. You'll find descriptions of a number of styles, from short essays to abstracts and process papers.

To get you going, we'll start out with the short papers. You may be asked to condense all your knowledge on a subject into a pithy essay or abstract, or even into a single paragraph. It's okay. Take a deep breath. You can do it, and here's how.

A Single Paragraph

The most important part of a single paragraph is its **topic sentence**, which contains the paragraph's main idea and is often (but not always) the first sentence. All the other sentences in the paragraph should support the topic sentence in some way. If they don't, cut them. Some ways to support your main idea are to elaborate, clarify, give details about, or provide proof for your topic sentence.

Some one-paragraph compositions also end with a summary sentence that restates, reviews, or emphasizes the main idea of the paragraph (using different words, of course).

Read this topic sentence:

▶ While April is the favorite time of year for many people, I dread it because my allergies are aggravated by blooming plants, I'm under a lot of pressure to get my taxes finished by the fifteenth, and I have to attend seven birthday parties for various family members.

After you read this topic sentence, you know that the rest of the paragraph will give you more details about the allergies, the tax-related pressure, and the birthday parties.

Don't forget to use transitional words or phrases within your paragraph. These help show your reader the connection between the various ideas you state or points you make.

The Five-Paragraph Essay

After single paragraphs, beginning writers often proceed to five-paragraph essays. These works follow a prescribed form of an introductory paragraph, three body paragraphs, and a concluding paragraph.

Just as a topic sentence is the main focus of a single paragraph, five-paragraph essays are centered around a **thesis statement** (or thesis sentence), the central view or argument of the whole essay. Your thesis statement may be either argumentative or informative, and it should be a summary of what the rest of your essay will contain. Make sure that your thesis statement is narrow enough to cover in a five-paragraph essay.

Your *introductory paragraph* should contain your thesis and also give a clear indication about what your body paragraphs will be about. (Some instructors or style guides mandate that your thesis statement be the first or last sentence of your introductory paragraph.) Your first paragraph should also include sentences that develop or build up to your thesis statement.

Your *body paragraphs* give more elaborate support for your thesis statement. Each of your body paragraphs should contain a topic sentence and must be directly related to your thesis statement. In other words, one subtopic (one individual point) can be developed in each of your three body paragraphs. Some writers find that they stay more focused if they list these three subtopics in their thesis statement. Read this example:

▶ I will no longer fly Zebra airlines because their online reservation system is not reliable, their support staff is not helpful, and their departures and landings are rarely on time.

From the thesis statement alone, readers know the first body paragraph will elaborate on the complaint about the reservation system, the second body paragraph will elaborate on the problems with the support staff, and the third body paragraph will elaborate on the unreliability of the schedules. Be sure that you word the points in your thesis statement in the same order as your body paragraphs and that you include transitions that tie together what you said in the preceding paragraph with the subtopic you're beginning in the next.

Your *concluding paragraph* is a summary of what you've stated in your body paragraphs (of course, with different wording). In this paragraph, you can recap the preceding paragraphs and give additional emphasis to your individual points. You should be careful not to introduce any new material in your concluding paragraph.

Some writers begin their concluding paragraph by restating their thesis statement in different words. Try starting out with the phrase *In conclusion* or *To summarize* (but delete the phrase after you finish your paragraph, as some readers find phrases like these to be trite).

The Abstract

In an **abstract** (usually written in just one paragraph), you summarize the methodology, essential sections, and main points (or conclusion) of research or a manuscript. By examining your abstract alone, readers should be able to determine what information the complete manuscript contains.

Different instructors, publications, and companies use different styles, but here are some general points:

- If you have a specific word limit, write as close as possible to that limit without going over it. Abstracts that exceed a specified word limit will often be rejected because they can't fit in certain databases or summary formats.
- Be sure you emphasize the primary discoveries and major conclusions of the work and include the key words of the research or work (that is what will be used in databases).
- Your wording should be as concise as possible and all irrelevant details should be omitted.

The Argument Essay

An **argument** is an essay in which you take a stance on a particular issue and expand on your point of view with supporting evidence. To construct an argument, first ask yourself what your main point is, then decide why that particular point is important. For instance, would a segment of society benefit if your stance were taken? Would certain problems be eradicated? Would money be saved?

Be sure to pursue some line of thought that's open to question—or else it's not an argument. In other words, you wouldn't write something like:

▶ Cotton candy is mostly made out of sugar.

That's because it's a simple statement of fact—there's nothing to argue. However, if you wrote that people should eat more cotton candy, you'd have a basis for debate and could proceed with an argument.

Give a lot of thought to the evidence you can give to support your point. If you can't think of several reasons your point is important (or if you can't find reasons through research), abandon that particular idea because you won't be able to support it well enough.

Note that the strength of an argument essay lies not only in the evidence provided by the writer to support his or her point, but in the writer's ability to anticipate opposing arguments and to objectively disprove them.

The Cause-and-Effect Essay

In a **cause-and-effect essay**, you examine the relationships between how certain events bring about or lead to other events. For instance, if you're looking at the causes of U.S. involvement in World War II, you'd write about the immediate cause (the bombing of Pearl Harbor) as well as causes that had been building up for some time (growing hostilities between the United States and Germany and the United States and Japan, increasing bonds between the United States and the Allies, and so on).

Be sure that there is actually a relationship between your suggested cause and effect. For instance, suppose you buy a new car and then two days later the dealership lowers the price on the model you bought. The dealership's sale had nothing to do with your previous purchase of the car, so there was no cause-and-effect relationship.

The following transition words and phrases can come in handy when writing a cause-and-effect essay: *accordingly, as a consequence, as a result, because, consequently, for this purpose, for that reason, hence, in order that, so, so that, then, therefore, thereupon, thus, to do this, to this end, with this in mind,* and *with this objective.*

Compare and Contrast

In a **comparison-and-contrast paper**, you record the similarities and the differences of people, places, events, and so on. Be sure to omit any statements of the obvious (e.g., Mercury and Mars are both planets that revolve around the sun).

Comparing and contrasting two people—or places or works—makes for an interesting or informative piece only if you look beyond what's readily apparent and describe or examine similarities and differences that your readers may not have been aware of or have thought about.

If an assignment calls only for comparison, make sure that you don't contrast—or vice versa. If the assignment calls for both, give each approximately the same amount of space.

The following transition words and phrases are useful for showing contrast: *after all, alternatively, although, and yet, at the same time, but, conversely, despite, even so, even though, for all that, however, in contrast, in spite of, instead, nevertheless, nonetheless, nor, notwithstanding, on the contrary, on the other hand, otherwise, regardless, still, though,* and *yet.*

Transition words and phrases of similarity include *again, also, and, as well as, besides, by the same token, for example, furthermore, in a like manner, in a similar way, in the same way, like, likewise, moreover, once more, similarly,* and *so.*

A Critical Analysis

In a **critical analysis**, you examine and assess a work from a number of points of view. Requirements often vary by instructor or company, but you should always include the following.

- Enough background information to familiarize your reader with the piece you're analyzing (including the name of the author or artist)
- A description of the way the piece was written
- The general thesis behind the piece or a synopsis of the work

The following list of questions may be helpful when composing a critical analysis.

- What biographical data about the author or artist is important?
- What are the purpose, tone, and format of the piece?
- How can the work be interpreted?
- Is there any information in the work that's inaccurate or incomplete?
- In what ways was the piece successful, and how did the author or artist achieve that success?
- In what ways did the author or artist fail?
- What could the author or artist have done to be more successful?
- Are there historical, psychological, geographical, gender, racial, cultural, or religious considerations that have an impact on the work?

If you're writing a critical analysis of a literary work, you need to consider points such as theme, symbolism, imagery, figurative language, setting, and characterization. Remember to avoid using the first-person point of view in a critical analysis unless your teacher, editor, or employer has specified that you may. In most instances, your personal like or dislike of a work would not be considered a suitable subject.

A Personal Journal

The material you write in a **journal** might be very personal or very detached—or anything in between. You might wish to use a journal just to record snippets of thoughts about work, or quotations that you find appealing or inspirational, or even the foods you eat every day—or you may choose to write about more personal experiences of your private life.

If you must keep a journal for a class, you might be given specific topics to reflect upon. In this case, be sure you understand whether your journal entries will be shared with others, and don't write anything that you feel is too personal (after all, you don't want the whole world to know your personal business!).

Descriptive Essays

An **essay of description** relies on imagery to be successful. Your readers are dependent on your words alone in order to see, hear, smell, taste, or feel your subject. For example:

▶ The unexpected spring storm sent sharp pellets of rain onto my face, forcing me to swallow the droplets as I panicked and screamed for help.

In this sentence, the reader can see, feel, and taste the rain, can hear the scream, and can therefore get a good picture of the narrator's predicament.

In a short story or novel, description of a setting helps readers feel closer to the characters or the plot because they can see and appreciate the characters' environment. In a nonfiction work, description helps readers know how a finished product should look (or feel, taste, smell, or sound).

Works of description rely on details, so be generous with them. Since description relates to as many of the senses as possible, use adjectives and adverbs liberally. In addition, take a look at the verbs you use and see if you can substitute ones that are more descriptive or precise. Instead of writing, "The man walked into the room," for example, give the reader a better look at how the man entered. Did he tiptoe into the room? bound? slink? prance? Now add adjectives and adverbs. Did the well-dressed man scurry into the room breathlessly? Did the seedy-looking man slink into the room furtively? Did the always-late man tiptoe into the room hesitantly?

While you should choose your descriptive words carefully, be careful not to overdo them. Keep in mind that every noun doesn't need an adjective (much less two or three) and every verb doesn't need an adverb.

Autobiographical Narratives

If you're writing an **autobiographical narrative** (sometimes called a personal narrative), you're telling a story about a noteworthy experience in your life. This type of story (usually written in the first person) revolves around an incident that made an impact in your life or taught you an important lesson.

Be sure to focus on a story that is not only important to you but also is valuable enough to be shared. The story of your exhilaration the first time you were behind the wheel of a car may be something you'd like to remember, but it alone would be boring for your readers. However, if you learned some valuable lesson (such as how you learned not to try to talk your way out of a speeding ticket) or an amusing anecdote (such as how you met your favorite movie star by accidentally crashing into his or her car on the freeway), then you have an incident that you can develop into an autobiographical narrative.

Be sure to add concrete details to explain and enhance your plot, setting, and characters. These will help you re-create the incident so your readers will stay involved in your story.

The Précis

A **précis** (pray-*cee*, from the French word for *precise*) is a clear and logical summary or abridgement of another author's work. Your précis should include the substance or general ideas put forth in the original work, but you must use your own words.

In writing a précis, you must:

- Identify the author's tone and point of view.
- Include the key words and major points of the original work.
- Include any valuable data that illustrates or supports the original work.
- Disregard any introductory or supplementary information.
- Use your own voice (you don't have to copy the original author's tone or voice).
- Not give your opinion of the author, the work, or the ideas presented.

In general, your précis should be no more than one-third the length of the original work you're summarizing. Remember that requirements (both of length and of format) vary with instructors, publishers, and companies, so be sure to check with them about what they specify.

The Process Paper

A **process paper** is a kind of how-to or explanation paper that explains a particular process by giving step-by-step directions or by describing certain changes or operations. Remember that a process paper must be written in chronological order.

For a process paper, it's important to define your audience, because they'll determine what kind of language you'll use and how much detail you'll go into. For instance, in a process paper about how to change a tire, you'd write in a less detailed manner for an audience of mechanics than you would for a group of beginning drivers.

If you're writing for a general audience, you need to explain anything that they might find confusing or unfamiliar. Think about how you would explain the process to children. Then reread your material and add a simple explanation of any words or concepts that children wouldn't be familiar with (without being patronizing!). Be sure to be precise when you give measurements. If you write "Use a little compost in the mixture," your readers may think that "a little" is a tablespoon, when you actually meant a gallon.

Remember that transition words and phrases help your reader see the chronological flow of the steps *(next, after that, finally)* as well as the placement of materials *(above, beside that, to the right)*.

Be sure to check with your instructor, publisher, or company about any mandates regarding point of view (usually a process paper is written in second person), use of bulleted lists, and use of illustrations, diagrams, or photos.

Business and Technical Writing

Works of **business and technical writing** often have many fine points specific to the field being discussed. The business you're writing for probably has particular styles that you're expected to use. In general, however, in business and technical writing, you should concentrate on five areas: *audience, clarity, conciseness, tone,* and *correctness.*

First, keep in mind who's going to receive your information. If you're writing for the general public, you'll probably need to take a different slant than if you're writing to a business associate. Sometimes you'll need to use a basic, "here-are-the-instructions" tone. Other times—for example, in business dealings—you'll need to be more formal.

Make sure that your writing is clear and concise. Use vocabulary that your audience will be familiar with. If you must introduce a word or concept that's unfamiliar to your audience, be sure to explain it in plain language.

After you've written your piece as clearly as possible, go back through it and see if there are any places you can shorten it. Your audience will read and remember a short piece more easily than they will a long one. Finally, be sure to check—and recheck and recheck—your spelling, punctuation, and word usage. You sure don't want something you wrote to be the latest joke around the water cooler.

The Research Paper

In a **research paper** you investigate a topic (often one that's been approved by an instructor or publisher) through consulting various sources, interpreting what the sources relate, developing ideas or conclusions, and citing the sources in your paper. A research paper might be one of the longest and (dare I say it?) most work-intensive pieces you'll ever have to write.

Research papers fall into one of two categories: *analytical papers,* which provide evidence that investigates and evaluates issues, or *argumentative papers,* which provide evidence to support your point of view and convince your readers that you're right. Research papers can be written in many formats; be sure that you know whether you're supposed to use a specific documentation style. The two most popular are the Modern Language Association (MLA) style, which is detailed in the *MLA Handbook for Writers of Research Papers,* and the American Psychological Association (APA) style, which is detailed in the *Publication Manual of the American Psychological Association.* Other books that you may be directed to use include:

- *The American Medical Association Manual of Style: A Guide for Authors and Editors,* by C. L. Iverson, A. Flanagin, P. B.

Fontanarosa, et al. (Baltimore, MD: Williams & Wilkins, 1998.)

- *The Chicago Manual of Style: The Essential Guide for Writers, Editors, and Publishers,* John Grossman (preface). (Chicago, IL: University of Chicago Press, 1993.)
- *Effective Writing: Improving Scientific, Technical, and Business Communication,* by Christopher Turk and John Kirkman. (New York, NY: E. & F.N. Spon, 1989.)
- *Form and Style: Research Papers, Reports, Theses,* by Carole Slade. (Boston, MA: Houghton Mifflin Company, 1999.)
- *Good Style: Writing for Science and Technology,* by John Kirkman. (New York, NY: Chapman & Hall, 1992.)
- *A Manual for Writers of Term Papers, Theses, and Dissertations,* by Kate L. Turabian. (Chicago, IL: University of Chicago Press, 1966.)
- *Scientific Style and Format: The CBE Manual for Authors, Editors, and Publishers,* by Edward J. Huth. (New York, NY: Cambridge University Press, 1994.)

Here are a few problems common to research papers to avoid:

- Topics that are too broad (for instance, "Jupiter: The Fifth Planet" or "Why Americans Enjoy the Cinema")
- Papers that don't adhere to specified page limits or word limits
- Papers that don't follow the directions about font size, font style, spacing, and margin size
- Papers that contain material that is plagiarized
- Citations that aren't written in the prescribed manner

Be sure you're aware of any timelines about material you must turn in before your actual paper is due. Some instructors give grades on different phases of writing a research paper like the following.

- Identification of your topic
- A preliminary proposal of your paper
- Your notes (sometimes required to be on cards of a specific size)
- An outline of your paper
- Various drafts of your paper
- Identification of bibliographic information and footnote style

The Review

While there are many ways to write a **review**, every way has this in common: you give your opinion about something and you also support or explain your opinion. Because you're writing a critical evaluation, not only do you have to mention both the noteworthy and the flawed aspects of your subject, you also have to explain what made them receive high or low marks.

Always keep your audience in mind. If you're reviewing a new restaurant, for instance, you'd probably need to give more explanation of unusual menu items to a general newspaper audience than you would to the readers of *Great Gourmet Goodies in America* magazine.

Your instructor, your company, or the publication you're writing for may mandate specific issues for you to address in your review. Take some time to read other reviews from magazines, newspapers, or scholarly papers that are written in a similar style and format.

Appendix A
1001 Frequently Misspelled Words

1. abdicate
2. absence
3. academically
4. accelerator
5. accessible
6. acclaim
7. acclimated
8. accommodate
9. accompanied
10. accomplish
11. accordion
12. accumulate
13. achievement
14. acknowledge
15. acoustics
16. acquaintance
17. acquitted
18. acute
19. adequately
20. adjacent
21. adjective
22. admission
23. admittance
24. adolescent
25. adultery
26. advantageous
27. adverb
28. advertisement
29. aerial
30. aerobic
31. aggravate
32. algebraic
33. alleged
34. allegiance
35. alliance
36. alliteration
37. allotting
38. almanac
39. already
40. altogether
41. amateur
42. ambassador
43. among
44. analogy
45. analysis
46. analyze
47. anecdote
48. angle
49. annihilate
50. annual
51. annul
52. antagonist
53. antithesis
54. apartheid
55. apartment
56. apologetically
57. apparatus
58. apparent
59. appearance
60. appositive

61. aptitude
62. arguing
63. argument
64. arrangement
65. ascend
66. aspirin
67. assessment
68. associative
69. assonance
70. asterisk
71. atheist
72. athletics
73. attendance
74. attitude
75. autumn
76. auxiliary
77. awfully
78. bachelor
79. balance
80. ballet
81. balloon
82. bankruptcy
83. barbarian
84. barbaric
85. barbecue
86. barbiturate
87. bargain
88. basically
89. battalion
90. bazaar
91. beautiful
92. beggar
93. beginning
94. behavior
95. beneficial
96. benefited
97. bilingual
98. biography
99. biscuit
100. bisect
101. bizarre
102. blasphemy
103. bologna
104. bookkeeper
105. bouillon
106. boulevard
107. boundary
108. boycott
109. bracelet
110. brackets
111. buffet
112. buoyant
113. bureaucrat
114. burial
115. calculation
116. camouflage
117. candidate
118. cantaloupe
119. caramel
120. caravan
121. carburetor
122. caricature
123. caring
124. cartographer
125. catalyst
126. catapult
127. catastrophe
128. category
129. cellar
130. centimeters
131. chagrined
132. challenge
133. changeable
134. changing
135. character
136. characteristic
137. chassis
138. chastise
139. chocolate
140. chord
141. chrome
142. chromosome
143. chunky
144. cigarette
145. cinnamon
146. circumference
147. circumstantial
148. citizen
149. cliché
150. climbed
151. cliques
152. coefficient
153. coherence

154. coincide
155. collectible
156. colonel
157. colony
158. colossal
159. column
160. coming
161. commingle
162. commission
163. commitment
164. committed
165. committee
166. communication
167. commutative
168. comparative
169. compatible
170. compelled
171. competent
172. competition
173. complementary
174. completely
175. complexion
176. composite
177. concede
178. conceit
179. conceivable
180. conceive
181. condemn
182. condescend
183. conferred
184. congratulations

185. congruent
186. conjunction
187. connoisseur
188. conscience
189. conscientious
190. conscious
191. consensus
192. consequences
193. consistency
194. consolidator
195. consonance
196. constitution
197. consumer
198. continuous
199. contraction
200. controlled
201. controller
202. controversial
203. controversy
204. convection
205. convenient
206. coolly
207. coordinates
208. corollary
209. corporation
210. correlate
211. correspondence
212. counselor
213. courteous
214. courtesy
215. criticism

216. criticize
217. crowded
218. crucifixion
219. cruelty
220. curriculum
221. curtail
222. cyclical
223. cylinder
224. dachshund
225. daughter
226. debacle
227. decadent
228. decagon
229. deceit
230. deep-seated
231. deferential
232. deferred
233. definitely
234. dependent
235. depose
236. descend
237. describe
238. description
239. desirable
240. despair
241. desperate
242. detrimental
243. devastation
244. develop
245. development
246. diagonal

247. diameter
248. dictionary
249. difference
250. dilettante
251. diligence
252. dimension
253. dining
254. disappearance
255. disappoint
256. disastrous
257. discipline
258. discrimination
259. disdainfully
260. disguise
261. dispel
262. dispensable
263. dissatisfied
264. disservice
265. distinguish
266. diversified
267. dormitory
268. drugged
269. drunkenness
270. easily
271. economy
272. ecosystem
273. ecstasy
274. efficiency
275. eighth
276. either
277. electrolyte
278. electromagnet
279. elegy
280. elevation
281. eligible
282. eliminate
283. ellipsis
284. embarrass
285. emigrate
286. eminent
287. emperor
288. emphasize
289. empire
290. employee
291. empty
292. enamel
293. encouragement
294. encouraging
295. endeavor
296. enemy
297. enormous
298. enthusiastically
299. entirely
300. entrance
301. equality
302. equator
303. equipped
304. espionage
305. espresso
306. essential
307. exaggerate
308. excellence
309. excess
310. exercise
311. exhaustion
312. exhibition
313. exhilarate
314. expansion
315. experience
316. experiment
317. exponent
318. expression
319. extinct
320. extraneous
321. extremely
322. extrovert
323. exuberance
324. factor
325. fallacious
326. fallacy
327. familiarize
328. fantasy
329. fascinate
330. fascination
331. fascism
332. favorite
333. feasible
334. federation
335. feisty
336. felicity
337. feminine
338. fiction

339. fictitious	370. guarantee	401. ignorance
340. financially	371. guerrilla	402. illogical
341. financier	372. guidance	403. imaginary
342. fiscal	373. gyration	404. imitate
343. fission	374. handicapped	405. immediately
344. fluent	375. happily	406. immigration
345. forcibly	376. harass	407. immortal
346. foreign	377. heinous	408. implement
347. foresee	378. heist	409. inaudible
348. foreshadowing	379. hemorrhage	410. incidentally
349. forfeit	380. heredity	411. incredible
350. formula	381. heritage	412. indicted
351. forty	382. heroes	413. indispensable
352. fourth	383. hesitancy	414. individually
353. frantically	384. hexagon	415. inequality
354. frequency	385. hierarchy	416. inevitable
355. fudge	386. hieroglyphics	417. influential
356. fulfill	387. hoping	418. information
357. fundamentally	388. horizontal	419. ingenious
358. galaxy	389. hospital	420. initially
359. gauge	390. humorous	421. initiative
360. genius	391. hygiene	422. innocent
361. geography	392. hyperbole	423. innocuous
362. government	393. hypocrisy	424. inoculate
363. governor	394. hypocrite	425. instantaneous
364. grammatically	395. hypotenuse	426. institution
365. grandeur	396. hypothesis	427. insurance
366. graphic	397. ideally	428. insurgency
367. grievous	398. idiom	429. intellectual
368. grizzly	399. idiomatic	430. intelligence
369. grocery	400. idiosyncrasy	431. intercede

432. interesting
433. interfered
434. interference
435. interjection
436. interminable
437. intermittent
438. interrogate
439. interrupt
440. intricate
441. introduce
442. introvert
443. invertebrate
444. irony
445. irrelevant
446. irresistible
447. irritable
448. isosceles
449. isthmus
450. jealousy
451. jewelry
452. journalism
453. judicial
454. jugular
455. kaleidoscope
456. kerosene
457. kindergarten
458. kinetic
459. laboratory
460. laborious
461. lapse
462. larynx

463. latitude
464. legitimate
465. length
466. lenient
467. liaison
468. library
469. license
470. lieutenant
471. lightning
472. likelihood
473. likely
474. limerick
475. lineage
476. liquefy
477. literature
478. llama
479. longitude
480. lose
481. lounge
482. lovely
483. luxury
484. lyric
485. magistrate
486. magnificence
487. mainland
488. maintain
489. malicious
490. manageable
491. manufacture
492. mariner
493. martyrdom

494. mass
495. mauve
496. meadow
497. mean
498. meanness
499. median
500. medieval
501. mediocre
502. melancholy
503. melodious
504. metallic
505. metaphor
506. mien
507. migratory
508. mileage
509. millennium
510. millionaire
511. miniature
512. minute
513. mischievous
514. misnomer
515. missile
516. misspelled
517. monarchy
518. mosquitoes
519. mundane
520. municipal
521. murmur
522. muscle
523. myriad
524. mysterious

525. myth
526. mythology
527. naïve
528. narcissism
529. narrative
530. nationalism
531. naturally
532. necessary
533. necessity
534. neighbor
535. neurotic
536. neutral
537. neutron
538. nineteen
539. ninety
540. ninth
541. nonpareil
542. noticeable
543. novelist
544. nowadays
545. nuclear
546. nucleus
547. nuisance
548. nutrition
549. nutritious
550. oasis
551. obedience
552. obsolete
553. obstacle
554. obtuse
555. occasionally
556. occurred

557. occurrence
558. octagon
559. official
560. omission
561. omitted
562. onomatopoeia
563. opaque
564. opinion
565. opossum
566. opponent
567. opportunity
568. oppose
569. opposition
570. oppression
571. optimism
572. optimistic
573. orchestra
574. orchid
575. ordinarily
576. origin
577. originate
578. outrageous
579. overrun
580. oxymoron
581. pageant
582. pamphlet
583. panicky
584. panorama
585. paradox
586. paralysis
587. paralyze
588. parenting

589. parliament
590. particular
591. pastime
592. patronage
593. pavilion
594. peaceable
595. peasant
596. pedestal
597. peers
598. penetrate
599. penicillin
600. peninsula
601. pentagon
602. perceive
603. performance
604. perimeter
605. permanent
606. permissible
607. permitted
608. permutation
609. perpendicular
610. perseverance
611. persistence
612. personal
613. personality
614. personification
615. personnel
616. perspiration
617. persuasion
618. pessimistic
619. pharaoh
620. pharmaceutical

621. phenomenon
622. Philippines
623. philosophy
624. physical
625. physician
626. picnicking
627. pilgrimage
628. pitiful
629. pixie
630. pizzazz
631. placebo
632. plagiarism
633. plagiarize
634. plague
635. planning
636. plausible
637. playwright
638. pleasant
639. pneumonia
640. politician
641. polygon
642. polyhedron
643. portray
644. Portuguese
645. possession
646. possessive
647. possibility
648. postscript
649. potato
650. potatoes
651. power
652. practically
653. prairie
654. precede
655. precedence
656. precipitation
657. precision
658. precocious
659. predicate
660. preference
661. preferred
662. prefix
663. prehistoric
664. premier
665. premiere
666. preparation
667. preposition
668. prescription
669. presence
670. prestige
671. presumption
672. prevalent
673. prime
674. primitive
675. prism
676. privilege
677. probability
678. probably
679. probation
680. procedure
681. proceed
682. professor
683. prognosis
684. prominent
685. pronounce
686. pronunciation
687. propaganda
688. propagate
689. protagonist
690. protein
691. proximity
692. psalm
693. psychoanalysis
694. psychology
695. publicly
696. pumpkin
697. pursue
698. puzzling
699. pyramid
700. pyrotechnics
701. quadrant
702. quadrilateral
703. quadruple
704. qualify
705. qualms
706. quandary
707. quantity
708. quarantine
709. quell
710. quench
711. querulous
712. query
713. quest
714. questionnaire
715. queue
716. quibble

717. quiescent
718. quinine
719. quintessentially
720. quipster
721. quizzes
722. quorum
723. quotation
724. quotient
725. radioactive
726. rampage
727. rampant
728. rampart
729. rarefy
730. ratio
731. realistically
732. realize
733. realtor
734. rebellion
735. recede
736. receipt
737. receive
738. receiving
739. reception
740. recession
741. reciprocals
742. recognize
743. recommend
744. rectify
745. reference
746. referred
747. referring
748. reflections

749. refraction
750. regiment
751. rehearsal
752. reign
753. reimburse
754. reincarnation
755. relieve
756. relieving
757. religious
758. remembrance
759. reminiscence
760. remittance
761. repetition
762. representative
763. repugnant
764. resemblance
765. reservoir
766. resistance
767. resources
768. responsibility
769. responsibly
770. restaurant
771. restoration
772. resume
773. retaliate
774. retrospect
775. reveal
776. rheumatism
777. rhombus
778. rhyme
779. rhythm
780. rhythmical

781. ridiculous
782. rotary
783. rotations
784. sacrifice
785. sacrilegious
786. safari
787. safety
788. salami
789. salary
790. sanitize
791. sarcasm
792. satellite
793. satire
794. saturate
795. scalene
796. scenery
797. schedule
798. scholastic
799. scrimmage
800. secede
801. sediment
802. segregate
803. segue
804. seismic
805. seismograph
806. seize
807. sensitive
808. sensory
809. sentry
810. sequence
811. sergeant
812. serpent

813. severely
814. shady
815. shameful
816. shanghai
817. shepherd
818. sherbet
819. sheriff
820. shining
821. shish kebab
822. shrewd
823. siege
824. significance
825. simian
826. similar
827. simile
828. siphon
829. situation
830. skeptical
831. skimp
832. skinned
833. soliloquy
834. sophomore
835. souvenir
836. spasmodic
837. specifically
838. specimen
839. sphere
840. sponsor
841. spontaneous
842. stalemate
843. stamen
844. statistic
845. statistics
846. statue
847. stimulus
848. stopped
849. straitjacket
850. strategy
851. strength
852. strenuous
853. stretch
854. stubbornness
855. studying
856. stupefy
857. subcontinent
858. submersible
859. subordinate
860. succeed
861. success
862. succession
863. sufficient
864. summary
865. summed
866. superintendent
867. supersede
868. supervisor
869. supplementary
870. supposed
871. supposition
872. suppress
873. surround
874. surroundings
875. susceptible
876. suspicious
877. sustenance
878. Swedish
879. swelter
880. syllable
881. symbolic
882. symmetrical
883. sympathy
884. symphonic
885. synchronize
886. syncopation
887. synonymous
888. synopsis
889. synthesize
890. syringe
891. tachometer
892. taciturn
893. talkative
894. tangent
895. tangible
896. tapestry
897. tariff
898. technical
899. technique
900. technology
901. temperamental
902. temperature
903. tenant
904. tendency
905. terminator
906. terrain
907. tertiary
908. themselves

909. theology
910. theoretical
911. theories
912. therefore
913. thermal
914. thermodynamic
915. thesaurus
916. thorough
917. though
918. thought
919. through
920. tolerance
921. tomorrow
922. tortoise
923. tournament
924. tourniquet
925. traffic
926. tragedy
927. transcend
928. transferring
929. transitory
930. transparent
931. trapezoid
932. tried
933. trough
934. trousers
935. truly
936. twelfth
937. tyranny
938. ukulele
939. unanimous
940. undoubtedly
941. universal
942. unmistakable
943. unnatural
944. unnecessary
945. unscrupulous
946. usually
947. utopian
948. vaccine
949. vacuum
950. vagabond
951. valedictory
952. valuable
953. variation
954. vaudeville
955. vehicle
956. vendor
957. veneer
958. vengeance
959. ventriloquist
960. venue
961. veracity
962. versatile
963. vestige
964. village
965. vinegar
966. violence
967. visage
968. visible
969. warrant
970. warring
971. warrior
972. watt
973. weather
974. welcome
975. wherever
976. whether
977. whisper
978. whistle
979. whittling
980. wholesome
981. withhold
982. woman
983. women
984. wreak
985. writing
986. written
987. wrongful
988. wrung
989. xylophone
990. yacht
991. yawn
992. yea
993. yeah
994. yuppie
995. zenith
996. zephyr
997. zinnia
998. zodiac
999. zoological
1000. zoology
1001. zucchini

Appendix B
Suggested Substitutes for Wordy Phrases

Wordy Phrase	Suggested Substitute
a considerable number of	many
a number of	some, several
adverse impact on	hurt, set back
affords the opportunity of	allows, lets
along the lines of	like
am of the opinion	think
are of the same opinion	agree
arrived at the conclusion	concluded
as a consequence	because
as a matter of fact	in fact
as a means of	to
ascertain the location of	find
at the present time	currently, now, today
at this point in time	now
based on the fact that	because
be aware of the fact that	know
came to a realization	realized
come to an agreement	agree
concerning the matter of	about, regarding
conduct an investigation (or) experiment	investigate, experiment

Wordy Phrase	**Suggested Substitute**
considering the fact that	because, since
despite the fact that	although, though
draw to your attention	to show, point out
each and every one	each, all
extend an invitation to	invite
for the reason that	because, since, why
give an indication of	show
has a requirement for	requires, needs
has the ability to, has the capacity for	can
if conditions are such that	if
in a position to	can, may, will
in addition to	besides, beyond, and, plus
in all likelihood (or) probability	likely, probably
in an effort to	to
in close proximity to	near, close, about
in large measure	largely
in light of the fact that	since, because
in spite of the fact that	although, despite
in the absence of	without
in the course of	during, while, in, at
in the event of (or) that	if
in the final analysis	finally
in the majority of instances	usually
in the midst of	during, amid
in the neighborhood of	near, close, about
in the very near future	soon
in this day and age	currently, now, today
in view of the fact that	because, since
is aware of the fact that	knows
it is imperative that we	we must
it is my understanding	I understand

Wordy Phrase	Suggested Substitute
it is often the case that	often
make a decision	decide
make a purchase	buy
make an application	apply
make an inquiry regarding	ask about, inquire about
notwithstanding the fact that	although
on the grounds that	because, since, why
one of the	a, an, one
owing to the fact that	because, since, why
place a major emphasis on	stress
take into consideration	consider
that being the case	therefore
the fact that	that
through the use of	through, by, with
to a certain degree	somewhat
under circumstances in which	when

Appendix C
Helpful Grammar and Writing Web Sites

Guide to Grammar and Writing
✐*http://ccc.commnet.edu/grammar/index.htm*
Information on grammar concepts with a number of interactive quizzes.

Grammar Bytes! Interactive Grammar Review
✐*www.chompchomp.com/menu.htm*
A list of grammar terms with interactive exercises on commas and irregular verbs.

FunBrain.com
✐*www.funbrain.com/spell/index.html*
A site for young students and parents with easy and hard spelling quizzes.

A Spelling Test
✐*www.sentex.net/~mmcadams/spelling.html*
A test of fifty difficult spelling words.

Reading from Scratch
✐*www.dyslexia.org/spelling_rules.shtml*
A list of rules that help teach spelling from the sounds letters make.

Bartleby.com
✐*www.bartleby.com*
An extremely helpful site that allows you to search a dictionary, encyclopedia, and thesaurus, as well as a number of guides to English usage and books of classic poetry and literature.

Merriam-Webster OnLine
✐*www.m-w.com/home.htm*
A searchable collegiate dictionary and thesaurus, along with a Word of the Day and interactive word games.

Index